Malpractice Depositions
Avoiding The Traps

Raymond M. Fish, **PhD, MD**
Melvin E. Ehrhardt, **MD, JD**

Medical Economics Books
Oradell, New Jersey 07649

Acquisitions Editor: Thomas Bentz
Production Editor: Dorothy Erstling
Text Design: Jayne Conte
Cover Design: Penina M. Wissner
Art Director: Sharyn Banks
Artist: Anthony Fischetto
Typesetting: Text Processing

Library of Congress Cataloging-in Publication Data

Fish, Raymond M.
    Malpractice depositions.

    Includes indexes.
       1. Depositions—United States.   2. Physicians—
Malpractice—United States. I. Ehrhardt, Melvin E.,
1941-   . II. Title. [DNLM: 1. Malpractice.
W 44 F532ma]

KF8900.F57 1986	346.7303'32'0269	86-8581
ISBN 0-87489-417-4	347.3063320269	

ISBN 0-87489-417-4

Medical Economics Company Inc.
Oradell, New Jersey 07649

Printed in the United States of America

CONTENTS

PUBLISHER'S NOTES

Raymond M. Fish, PhD, MD, has served both as expert medical witness in court and as a consultant in planning and developing defenses against malpractice charges. A fellow of the American College of Emergency Physicians, he practices at the Burnham City Hospital Trauma Center in Champaign, Illinois, and is clinical instructor in emergency medicine at the University of Illinois, Champaign-Urbana. He is adjunct professor of electrical and bioengineering at the University of Illinois, and has designed a cardiotachometer for the NASA Manned Spacecraft Center and invented an audio instrument for the US Public Health Service that lets the blind "see" in two dimensions. He is coauthor with Melvin E. Ehrhardt, MD, JD, and Betty Fish, MSW, of *Malpractice: Managing Your Defense* (Medical Economics Books, 1986).

Melvin E. Ehrhardt, MD, JD, director of emergency care at Mennonite Hospital, Bloomington, Illinois, has taught clinical and medicolegal course at the University of Illinois, and written on medical evidence, malpractice, and legal implications in surgery, and computer programs on informed consent and abuse. He has led in-service training for physicians and attorneys, consulted in legal preparation, and served as an expert witness in malpractice court cases.

Herbert H. Kauffman, whose passing preceded publication of this book, edited this text with the mastery and integrity he maintained as chief copy editor of *Medical Economics* magazine.

ACKNOWLEDGMENTS

Many people helped make this book possible. Some told us of their experiences, some directed us to relevant literature, and others reviewed the manuscript itself. Paul Fish, JD, and Alan Baird, MD, deserve special mention. Our gifted editor, the late Herb Kauffman, pulled it all together with clarity and grace.

Others we wish to thank for their assistance include Mary Lee Cascio, RN; Rubin Cohn, JD; Eileen Felkner, RN; James Kearns, JD; Jamie Perry, RN; James D. Rogers, MD; The Honorable Judge Robert Steigman, JD; and Van Tetidrick, RN.

INTRODUCTION

Only a small fraction of medical malpractice cases go to court. The rest are settled out of court after some amount of fact-finding. The most important fact-finding occurs during the deposition, when the defendant physician tells the opposition what happened in the case. Sworn testimony is given during the deposition, and it can be used later in court, although the information is usually used to facilitate a settlement—but don't count on that.

The deposition verifies the accuracy of the medical record and other documents. Some of the major difficulties the physician will face in a deposition are summed up by New York attorney Stuart A. Summit (*The Deposition: A Simulation With Commentary*, the American Bar Association Section of Litigation and Young Lawyers Division, 1978, American Bar Association, p 110): "Being a witness is a highly artificial business for which there is no adequate background or experience...Testifying at an oral deposition is the most artificial process of all. The witness will think he is participating in an essentially oral event—he will be questioned and must answer. That impression is dangerous. A deposition is a process by which a document is prepared, and nothing else. All that matters is the transcript.

"Think of it! A lawyer or business executive faced with having to prepare an important writing will consider what he wants to say and will draft and edit until he is satisfied. He may seek the opinion of others before he permits the document to be made final...But the witness at the deposition is given no such opportunity. No matter how much he prepares before he enters the deposition room, he cannot know what questions will be asked. . .."

Many trial attorneys spend a significant percentage of their time in depositions. The physician wanting advice on how to handle a deposition in a malpractice case may find a few short articles on the subject, but that is about all. Yet the information is buried in the legal literature and between the lines in deposition transcripts. We've studied all material and—plus our own personal experiences—are prepared to help deal with the many traps encountered during malpractice depositions.

We'll discuss how to prepare for and deal with the opposition's time-consuming, confusing, upsetting, and potentially damaging deposition tactics. You'll also learn about the importance of other people's depositions—and how all the depositions in your case may support your claim in a countersuit.

1

YOUR DEPOSITION IS A
DANGEROUS EXPERIENCE

You can easily lose your malpractice case during the deposition, a meeting in which your patient's attorney questions you in order to get information that will support the claim of malpractice. The deposition, which is under the jurisdiction of the court handling your malpractice case, is a critically important part of most malpractice cases. This chapter describes how a deposition must be conducted, who may attend it, what can be discussed, and the risks for the physician defendant.

THE KEY TO EARLY SETTLEMENT

Most malpractice cases are settled out of court. One large malpractice insurer, the Illinois State Medical Inter-Insurance Exchange, found that, between 1976 and 1984, only 3 percent of all cases went to trial.

Plaintiff's attorneys often want to settle a case early because it is time-consuming and expensive to prepare a case for trial—and a jury trial can be risky. If a plaintiff (the patient) has a valid claim, it is to his or her advantage to settle the claim quickly. Most malpractice claims are settled within two years of when they are filed, which is usually about four years after the alleged negligence took place.[1] But depositions and related activities can complicate matters.

SOME CASES DRAG
ON FOR YEARS

In one case several years ago (Sue Brown, His malpractice coverage fell $2.4 million short, *Medical Economics*, July 25, 1983, p 54-57), papers were filed to initiate a malpractice suit two years after the negligence occurred. The defense attorneys complained that they could not come to trial because the opposing counsel had not given them the autopsy report and other medical data needed to prepare the defense. Two years later, the plaintiff's lawyers complained that the physician's lawyer was withholding records of the examination of the patient. A year later, the physician's attorney said that he had not received all of the patient's medical history. The defense also wanted to receive the patient's tax records and earnings statements.

The case was finally scheduled for a court hearing six and a half years after the alleged negligence occurred. However, the patient's attorney was trying a case in another city at that time, and one of his expert witnesses had died. They needed time to find a replacement. Three years later, the case was again scheduled to go to court.

The physician lost the jury trial. The physician's attorneys prepared an order asking the judge who heard the case to reduce the award or overturn the verdict. The order was on the judge's desk on the day he died. The judgment against the physician was $2.6 million. However, $2 million in interest was charged because of the nine years that had gone by since the alleged negligence (the law does not allow such interest in many states). Regrettably, the physician had only $2 million in malpractice insurance.

Moral: A decade is a long time to have the possibility of financial ruin hang over one's head. Fortunately, depositions in most malpractice cases bring things to conclusion much sooner.

Settlements are made on the basis of information gathered, or "discovered" about the case. The process of discovery includes examining the plaintiff's losses or disability, collecting physical evidence relevant to the case, and questioning people who know about the case during depositions.

Nurses, members of the patient's family, medical experts, and others may be questioned in a deposition. Nothing is more useful to a plaintiff's attorney, however, than statements you make that support the claim of malpractice. Whether or not the malpractice claim has merit, attorneys can make you look negligent by using a variety of tactics and techniques.

IS DEPOSITION MANDATORY?

Not always. A physician came to one of us while this book was being written. Her malpractice case was coming to trial in a few months. Many other people involved in the suit had already given depositions. She was upset that, as far as she knew, no deposition was planned for her. She was concerned that she would not be able to explain her side of the case.

We told her that she would be fortunate if she could avoid being deposed: During the deposition the opposition would learn her defenses and explanations for what happened in the case and would then have time to think of reasons why the explanations were inadequate. She would be better off if she went to the settlement table or court with her knowledge of the case and defenses unknown to the opposition. We convinced the physician not to be concerned about demanding the right to be deposed.

In practice, however, most physicians being sued are forced to undergo the unpleasant and dangerous experience of being "deposed."

THE TRIAL LAWYER'S "DEADLY WEAPON"

Some people feel that a strong showing at a deposition will make the opposition back down. This does happen, but don't count on it. Listen to these experts:

- "Depositions are the most deadly weaons in the arsenal of the trial lawyer...Most trial lawyers spend the majority of their time not in court trying lawsuits, but, in fact, in the taking of depositions before trial."[2]
- "Of all the discovery methods...It is only the oral deposition which permits the spontaneity and conflict necessary for testing perceptions by follow-up questions and immediate inquiry into peripheral matters. Most importantly, it is the only opportunity to obtain admissions directly from parties, rather than from the written words of attorneys. It provides a chance to determine the credibility and demeanor of a witness and the impression he or she is likely to create upon the jury. Under most circumstances in the personal injury case the oral deposition should be the focal point of the discovery plan. All other discovery devices should be utilized, at least partially, for deposition preparation."[3]

That's why your deposition is dangerous. The opposition can pry much useful—and harmful—information out of you.

YOUR RIGHTS UNDER THE LAW

The Federal Rules of Civil Procedure is the established legal reference that describes how depositions are to be conducted. It defines the law in federal courts and in some state courts as well. The individual states adopt most of the federal rules and their amendments.

State laws and local customs vary, and your attorney should be familiar with them. The federal rules are quoted in several places in this book because they are the basis of most state laws. The quotes describe your rights and responsibilities in depositions. Read them carefully.

WHAT THE PLAINTIFF'S ATTORNEY REALLY WANTS TO KNOW

The goal of the plaintiff's attorney at your deposition is to obtain information that will prove your negligence. During a deposition you should cooperate fully with the questioning, as long as the questioning is done properly. Don't, however, provide more information than necessary under the law.

Here are the types of information the plaintiff's attorney will try to get during the deposition to prove your negligence:

1. Information you swear is true, facts about the case, admissions, material for impeachment.
2. How you plan to deny the charge of negligence (i.e., the theory of the defense).
3. What medical references and experts are to be used by the defense.
4. What additional evidence, proofs, and theories are needed to prove the patient's case.
5. Whether or not proof will be needed to show that the plaintiff's evidence is authentic.
6. How good a witness you will be, and your ability to think under pressure and look impressive to a jury.
7. The names of possible additional witnesses and defendants.
8. The prospects for a settlement.

Information and statements you make will be sworn to when you sign the deposition transcript. Your statements recorded in the transcript can be read at the settlement table and, if the case goes that far, to the jury at your trial. If you are not careful during the long, complex hours of deposition testimony, what you say can be used to do several things: destroy your credibility, show your prejudice or bias, contradict your previous or future statements, demonstrate that your memory is inaccurate, show that your testimony is based on what your attorney coached you to say rather than your memory of events, and prove the patient's case.

Getting you to admit during a deposition that evidence is correct can relieve the patient's attorney of the expensive and time-consuming task of proving the authenticity of the evidence. So don't admit to anything that may not be true. You will be asked whether information and evidence is authentic: X-rays, chart entries, content of alleged conversations, and the occurrence of disputed events. Will you confirm the information, or must the patient's attorney prove it?

Example: Relatives may claim that you were no longer friendly or concerned about the patient when you found that bills were not being paid. If you do not dispute the claim when it is brought up during the deposition, the opposition will no longer have the difficult task of proving the accusation.

However, you need to be reasonable in verifying the authenticity of documents or other evidence. The Federal Rule of Civil Procedure does consider the unreasonable failure to verify the authenticity of evidence in Rule 37(c): "If a party fails to admit the genuineness of any document or the truth of the matter, he may apply to the court for an order requiring the other party to pay him the reasonable expenses incurred in making that proof, including reasonable attorney's fees. The court shall make the order unless it finds that (1) the request was held objectionable. . .or (2) the admission sought was of no substantial importance, or (3) the party failing to admit had reasonable ground to believe that he might prevail on the matter, or (4) there was other good reason for the failure to admit."

HOW GOOD A WITNESS ARE YOU?

During your deposition, the opposition will discover this. Can you think on your feet, understand questions, make a good impression on listeners, and keep your temper? If you're evasive or halting, the deposition will suggest to the patient's attorney that he can prove you to be dishonest and uncooperative.

In some depositions, the opposition may try, through questioning, to show how you were responsible for the damages; this might lead to a settlement. In other depositions, the plaintiff's strategy is to extract as much data as possible while revealing as little as possible.[4] You will be in a better position to cope with such tactics after you have discussed the case with your medical experts and heard the depositions of others in the case.

Caution: Try to avoid giving deposition before you have hired one or more expert witnesses. Try to be among the last to be deposed.

TIP-OFFS FROM PLAINTIFFS' ATTORNEYS

One legal text suggests that plaintiff's attorneys use the following steps for analyzing and using depositions:

1. Prepare a summary of the contents of the deposition, including notes about the demeanor and credibility of the witness.
2. Prepare a detailed index. The court reporter sometimes prepares an index, but this would not be detailed enough for use.
3. Mark the text of the deposition in the margins with suggestions on how specific questions and answers will be used at a trial, noting especially: admissions, cross-examination topics, specific impeachment material, objectionable questions and answers, and other responses to be used or read into the evidence at the trial.[5]

One attorney sums it up this way: "The defendants have control of the facts. It follows from that basic axiom that the case will have to be tried along lines that assume that the events are as the defendant describes them. Taking the events as the defendant describes them, you must prove that his treatment failed to meet minimally acceptable standards of practice. Sometimes, because of naiveté, arrogance, or poor preparation, or a combination of these factors, the defendant, at the deposition, will have so incriminated himself that there is no defense left available. More frequently, no such happy circumstance will occur. At a minimum, however, you wish to build fences through which he cannot escape. . . ."[6]

In other words, beware! Think of how important your words are and how they will be analyzed.

WHO MAY BE PRESENT AT YOUR DEPOSITION

The attorneys or the court reporter may decide who can be present at your deposition, depending on local laws and customs. In general, depositions should not be open to the public or the press. Because information revealed may be objected to as being irrelevant or privileged, the public has no right to learn of such information. Deposition questioning may delve into much information that will be inadmissable at trial.

Tip: You can request that persons attending a deposition be identified and that their presence be noted on the record.

The Federal Rules of Civil Procedure states that the court may decide who can be present at a deposition, taking into consideration annoyance and embarrassment of the parties involved. Your defense attorney should be familiar with Rule 26(c). It's important because it specifies the types of protective orders your attorney may request of the court when you find your deposition being conducted in an unreasonable manner.

The patient and other persons who are involved in the case may be present at your deposition. Some witnesses are hesitant to speak badly of another person when that person is present. But don't you be intimidated.

Example: Don't be afraid to say that the patient often did not take medication because he or she was drunk. Speak the truth whether or not the patient is present.

You may be distracted by large numbers of observers, paralegals, the patient's relatives, and attorneys at your deposition. If so, ask your attorney to object to them being there. If the request is not granted, don't put up with noise, gestures, interruptions, smoking, or other disturbances from the spectators. If you are unsuccessful in making unnecessary persons leave, pause each time there is a disturbance and wait until it is over. You deserve respect and want to make sure the court reporter can hear what you are saying.

Expert witnesses hired by the opposition may be present at your deposition. Don't get involved in trying to decide if the sudden frown on the expert's face means that your medical knowledge is incorrect. The frown may mean that you know too much. Or the frown may be deliberately made to confuse you. Just be prepared to speak knowledgeably about your subject, whether or not the experts are present at your deposition.

The patient's attorney may bring paralegals or other attorneys to help with the paperwork, take messages, and get food and drink. This second set of eyes, ears, and legs enables the opposition to concentrate on the questioning and simultaneously be looking up laws, facts about the case, and previous testimony. You are at a disadvantage.

In contrast to having trained assistants helping with multiple tasks to make the deposition run favorably, in a deposition you may be overwhelmed and worried about your patients, office, family, insurance rates, and reputation. If you recognize how such thoughts can put you at a disadvantage, you can concentrate on what's significant in your deposition.

WHAT YOU CAN BE ASKED IN THE DEPOSITION

You must answer questions that might reasonably be expected to lead to the discovery of admissible evidence. The often-quoted rule that permits attorneys to question you so freely is Rule 26(b)(1) of the Federal Rules of Civil Procedure. This quote is worth reading several times until it is understood, because it defines exactly what physicians find themselves being questioned about in malpractice depositions.

". . .Parties may obtain discovery regarding any matter, not privileged, which is relevant to the subject matter involved in the pending action, whether it relates to the claim or defense of the party seeking discovery or to the claim or defense of any other party, including the existence, description, nature, custody, condition, and location of any books, documents, or other tangible things and the identity and location of persons having knowledge of any discoverable matter. It is not ground for objection that the information sought will be inadmissible at the trial if the information sought appears reasonably calculated to lead to the discovery of admissible evidence."

Federal Rule 26(b)(1) goes on to set limits on these broad powers given to the plaintiff's attorney who will question you: "The frequency or extent of use of the discovery methods set forth. . .shall be limited by the court if it determines that: (i)the discovery sought is unreasonably cumulative or duplicative, or it is obtainable from some other source that is more convenient, less burdensome, or less expensive; (ii) the party seeking discovery has had ample opportunity by discovery in the action to obtain the information sought; or (iii) the discovery is unduly burdensome or expensive, taking into account the needs of the case, the amount in controversy, limitations on the parties' resources, and the importance of the issues at stake in the litigation. The court may act upon its own initiative after reasonable notice or pursuant to a motion. . . ."

Under Rule 26, you can be forced to bring all records, notes, charts, X-rays, and anything else that might reasonably be expected to lead to the discovery of evidence that would be admissible in court. Thus, even if a document would be considered confidential, prejudicial, or otherwise objectionable in court, you can be asked to produce it at the deposition.

Example: The notes your attorney sent to an expert witness to tell about your case can be examined by the patient's attorney.

Reminder: Broad rules of discovery reduce the number of cases that go to court. Both sides have the ability to learn what the other knows about the case. A settlement often results when both sides know each other's strengths and weaknesses.

SPEAK OPENLY TO YOUR ATTORNEY

While preparing for your deposition, remember that you may reveal information about your patient during the deposition and in court—but not elsewhere. To this extent, your patient has lost the benefit of the physician-patient confidentiality by suing you. One of the few things you can refuse to answer about during your deposition are the privileged communications you have had with your attorney. However, the *facts* you discuss don't become privileged or secret just because you talked about them with your attorney. And if you use written notes derived from conversations with your attorney to refresh your memory before a deposition, the opposition may be able to force you to surrender these notes. While what you say to your attorney is privileged, the fact that you had conferences with him isn't privileged in some jurisdictions. Also, if other people were present during your meetings, the content of your discussions may be discoverable.

Don't be afraid of being asked during your deposition about preparing your case with your attorney. You can answer confidently and honestly, "Of course, I reviewed the case with my attorney." There is no reason for shame or intimidation. Naturally you'll avoid saying that your attorney coached you or told you what to say. If asked what your attorney told you to say, reply, "He told me to tell the truth."

REMEMBER, THE OPPOSITION CAN CROSS-EXAMINE YOU

Leading questions, though confusing, are permitted. The scope of the inquiry is wider than at trial: The possibility that information may lead to admissible evidence, rather than admissibility of the information itself, will determine whether or not the information can be discussed with you.

During your deposition, you may be asked questions about what constitutes proper treatment. Such questions are usually asked of an expert witness. Though your attorney may object to such questions, you may need to answer them. Some courts have recognized the right of the plaintiff's attorney to question the physician as if he were an expert witness.[7] The landmark case in this regard is McDermott v. Manhattan Eye, Ear, and Throat Hospital (15 NY 2d 23; 255 NYS 2d 65).

OBJECTIONS DURING THE DEPOSITION

Your attorney will make objections to some of the questions you are asked. You won't understand the reasons for many of the objections made during a deposition. Some are made as a signal to warn you that a trap has been set; you must be careful. Certainly don't answer until your attorney tells you to. If an objection is made because a question is unclear or ambiguous, this should immediately be correctable: The patient's attorney will reword the question.

Even though your attorney objects to a question, you may be required to answer it. Some courts have ruled that an attorney has no right to instruct a witness to refuse to answer a question during a deposition. If an objection is made, the question can later be stricken from the transcript if the objection is upheld. If objections interfere with the questioning, it is possible for the patient's attorney to conduct the deposition before a magistrate who will rule on objections as they arise.

Tell your attorney to state the reasons for objections during a deposition in a way you can understand. Then, even if he can't instruct you not to answer a question, he can hint to you as to why the question is improper.

Example: Your attorney might object to a question, stating that the question is ambiguous as to time. You would then state that you are unable to answer the question because of the vague time frame.

CONCLUSIONS

Many physicians don't realize that the malpractice deposition is a trap. Though you can't avoid spending some time in a deposition, you can avoid being permanently caught by it. The ground rules concerning depositions are complex and vary from state to state, but the basic process is the same.

The tangible result of the deposition that can be used to prove your negligence is the deposition transcript—the subject of our next chapter.

REFERENCES

1. *Malpractice Lifeline.* vol 4, no 2, Feb 26, 1979.
2. Luvera PN: *How to take a deposition,* Personal Injury Annual. Matthew Bender & Co, 1981.
3. Stein SB: Oral depositions in federal civil practice, in Miller DG: *Taking and defending depositions in personal injury cases.* Practicing Law Institute, 1983, pp 27-64.
4. Werchick A: Deposing the doctor defendant, in Miller DG: *Taking and defending depositions in personal injury cases.* Litigation and Administrative Practice Series Litigation Course Handbook Series No 236, Practicing Law Institute, pp 91-109.
5. Haydock RS, Herr DF: *Discovery Practice.* Boston, Little Brown & Co, 1982.
6. Shandell RE: *The preparation and trial of medical malpractice cases.* New York, Law Journal Seminars Press, 1981.
7. Passman A: Discovery techniques in malpractice cases, in Davis PA: *Discovery Techniques: A Handbook for Michigan Lawyers.* Ann Arbor, The Institute of Continuing Legal Education, Hutchins Hall, 1977, chap 37-42.

2

HOW TO HANDLE YOUR DEPOSITION TRANSCRIPT

If the patient's attorney has his way, the deposition transcript will prove your negligence. The transcript describes what was said and done during the deposition. Your testimony during the deposition can later be taken out of context and quoted, so it is important that the transcript accurately reflect what you are trying to say. You must maintain your right to review, correct, and sign it.

Action: Obtain deposition transcripts from recent malpractice cases in your area to see how depositions are conducted. If possible, obtain copies of transcripts in which your patient's attorney did the questioning.

VIRTUALLY EVERYTHING WILL BE TRANSCRIBED

In general, everything said during the deposition will be recorded. If the plaintiff's and the defense attorney both request that a conversation be "off the record," the request will be honored. If only one side of the case wants a conversation to be off the record, the request will not be honored.

At times both sides will agree to go "off the record" to have a discussion. After the discussion is over and transcription has started, the plaintiff's attorney may recite into the record what was said in the off-the-record discussion! Or he may demand that you say what transpired during an unofficial discussion with your attorney. These nasty tricks are considered proper because, under the law, any possibly relevant information is discoverable. So, take a walk or whisper away from microphones when consulting with your attorney. Claim that your conversation was privileged if pushed to disclose what was said.

Reminder: If the patient's attorney overhears you make a comment before the deposition begins or during a recess, you can be made to repeat the comment for the record. Similarly, off-hand remarks or comments you make may be recorded.

THE BIG RISKS IN JOKING

Lawyers sometimes repeat in court jokes physicians have made off the record before or after a deposition. The atmosphere may be relaxed, and everyone may be joking, but they are out to get you. Many of us in medicine have a strong desire to be liked by those around us, and joking is how we satisfy part of that need. Realize that such behavior is inappropriate around lawyers—in the deposition or not! Don't tell jokes.

And don't laugh at jokes told by the opposition. Just act like you didn't hear anything. If asked what you think about a joke or off-color comment, refuse to speak—coldly ignore the request if you are not being officially questioned.

If during official questioning you are asked inappropriate or embarrassing material (e.g., "Women with small breasts are unattractive, don't you think?"), say you don't understand the question or you have no opinion on the matter. Keep saying you don't understand or you have no opinion no matter how many times the question is rephrased. The question is a trap.

In sum: Avoid even the mildest obscenity, ethnic slur, derogatory comment, or joke of any kind. You are under oath during the deposition, and there is no such thing as being off the record.

WHAT YOU NEED TO KNOW ABOUT COURT REPORTERS

A court reporter types the deposition transcript. Usually the accuracy of the transcription is nearly perfect, word for word. However, one of us took part in a medical arbitration hearing that was being recorded by a "court reporter." The transcript was so poorly done that both parties agreed it was worthless.

Some reporters will edit out meaningless words such as "Well, uh, let's see now," especially if they were made by an attorney. Usually, statements of deponents aren't so freely edited.

If the reporter is being paid by the plaintiff's attorney, the reporter might take orders from that attorney preferentially, though in practice this is almost unheard of. Rule 28(c) of the Federal Rules of Civil Procedure states "Disqualification for Interest. No deposition shall be taken before a person who is a relative or employee or attorney or counsel of any of the parties, or is a relative or employee of such attorney or counsel, or is financially interested in the action." The parties in an action can overrule this restriction by written agreement covered in Rule 29, as when the defense agrees that the plaintiff's attorney's secretary can be the reporter.

Tell your attorney long before the deposition if you're concerned about the opposition hiring a biased reporter. Practically all reporters are fair, but the plaintiff's attorney could selectively use one of those very few who aren't. The reporter must make subjective judgments, as when putting comments in the record concerning unfair treatment befalling one party or another. For example, if the patient's attorney is shouting at you, the defense attorney should request that this be put in the record. Conversations held "off the record" may—erroneously or not—be kept in the transcript. The court reporter may "inadvertently" exaggerate the length of pauses before a witness responds by describing them as being "long."

Your unspoken responses may not be properly interpreted by the reporter. Shaking the head Yes or No and indicating size with arm movements may unwittingly go unnoticed. Such actions delay the proceedings and lead to confusion. When an unspoken answer is missed by the reporter, the plaintiff's attorney can later claim that the question was not answered.

Don't rush: Don't speak too quickly during your deposition. One physician, who had given expert evidence during a malpractice deposition, noted that two pages of transcript were completely jumbled in such a way as to reverse his evidence. In practical terms, so much material was incorrectable. The physician had no reason to believe the court reporter was partial to the plaintiff's attorney. Then the physician remembered that he'd spoken far too quickly during that part of his testimony.

WHERE TO LOOK WHEN SPEAKING

It is polite, natural, and helpful to look at the person speaking to you. Don't keep looking at the reporter, although you should occasionally look at her to see that your words are being followed and to remind yourself that you are making a legal document. The reporter shouldn't be at your back because she must be able to hear your every word.

BE AWARE OF DEPOSITION EXHIBITS

"Exhibits" may be described in the deposition transcript and labeled as evidence. Exhibits include X-rays, medical records, and drawings you make in explaining yourself. If you're not an excellent artist, refuse to draw diagrams for the opposition. Say truthfully that you're not capable of drawing meaningful or accurate pictures in a short time.

Any pictures you do draw will be kept as evidence. If they're not expertly done (and even if they are), they may be brought to court and held next to a professional drawing that could look very different. This, of course, would be done to make you look unskilled or foolish in front of the jury.

Even notes you carry to the deposition can be demanded from you and described in the transcript. If you bring anything in your briefcase or pockets, the opposition has the right to take them. After all, everything that may lead to information about the case is "discoverable."

Moral: There are many precautions you must take to prevent inaccurate and embarrassing information from being recorded in the deposition transcript.

WHAT YOU SAY CAN BE TAKEN OUT OF CONTEXT

You will be held to what you say in the deposition, although you can correct the transcript in various ways as described later. Statements can be taken out of your deposition transcript to be combined, compared, and analyzed. Many plaintiff's (patient's) attorneys index depositions as to subjects covered; they don't just *read* what you said.

The following quote from a recent malpractice deposition shows the unorganized, unsure thinking of a physician. She was either confused or trying to cut the deposition short by answering a question incompletely, and therefore inaccurately. At first she seemed to not know how a doctor determines the proper endotracheal tube size to use in any given patient. Later she did describe a definite formula for determining endotracheal tube size. However, she did initally say that she "guesses" at the size.

If this admission had been left as it was, it would be valuable for the plaintiff's case at the bargaining table or in front of a jury. In this deposition, the plaintiff's attorney mercifully pointed out the oversimplification to the doctor, who then corrected her testimony:

Plaintiff's attorney: How do you select the proper sized endotracheal tube?

Doctor: There are no set standards. You have a rough idea; you make a guess that a certain size will fit the patient.

Plaintiff's attorney: This is done by guesswork?

Doctor's attorney: I don't think she said she guesses at the size.

Plaintiff's attorney: Let the reporter read what the doctor's answer was. . . .. (After the reading): The doctor did say "guess."

Doctor: I used the wrong word. What I meant was a calculation, not a guess. Actually it's rather complicated. But what you do, if you want to get technical, is to add 18 to a person's age. Up to the age of 18 years. So, if a person is 18 years or older, you use a size 36 endotracheal tube. The size of the person does influence the actual decision, however, so there are other subjective influences in the size determination.

Moral: Be thoughtful and organized in your speaking so that you don't make statements that could be taken out of context to embarrass you. Don't oversimplify.

THE DANGERS IN VIDEOTAPING THE DEPOSITION

Videotapes were used in a trial in which a dead man won a malpractice suit against a dead physician. The patient had testified on a videotape that had been made shortly before he died. His widow was awarded $600,000 because the deceased physician had failed to diagnose the patient's terminal cancer. The tape was held in a court vault until the time of the trial.[1]

Audio and videotapes of depositions have often been used when a person won't be able to come to court. Another advantage: A jury in the midst of long days of courtroom testimony will perk up when a TV set is placed in front of them. They will take note of what they see.

But unless you won't be available for the trial, you must refuse to allow your deposition to be videotaped. There are several dangers in being videotaped. A statement read from a deposition transcript is generally thought of as coming out of a larger discussion. On the other hand, people are used to short TV news reports that supposedly give the most important information briefly. A jury might react that way—negatively.

Another problem with being videotaped is that people are used to seeing good-looking, relaxed people on the TV screen. Even if you do look like a movie star in the morning, you probably won't after five hours of questioning. A TV camera is likely to catch the strain and discomfort associated with answering questions under pressure. Strained facial expressions may induce distrust in the jury.

BOX 2-1

Things to Avoid If You Do Have to be Videotaped

1. Activities that interfere with sound pickup: not facing the microphone; tapping the microphone or table it sits on; jiggling coins in one's pocket; moving chairs or papers while someone is talking; and street or office sounds in the background.

2. Things that interfere with picture pickup: not facing the camera and improper lighting (e.g., the sun shining through a window behind you).

3. Attempting to show things that aren't seen well on the screen (unless expertly produced): details on X-rays and scars (though shadows may exaggerate rather than hide scars).

And what about lighting and catching your face at proper angles? Professional cameramen have a difficult time with this in studios. And it would be difficult to find a TV personality willing to go on camera without a professional makeup job to make him look just right. So, if possible, avoid the camera.

If you *are* videotaped, however, avoid the risks listed in the accompanying table. These things would make a videotape of your deposition less acceptable for jury viewing.

SIGNING THE DEPOSITION TRANSCRIPT

You will be asked to check the deposition transcript for accuracy and sign it. Then you will have sworn to its accuracy. If anything you said in the transcript is later proven to be untrue or inconsistent with future statements you make, you will have been proved a liar.

So it's important that you check the accuracy of the deposition.

Correct stenographic errors; watch for tiny grammatical errors that change the sense of what you said.

But how are you to remember what was said during hours of conversation? It's a good idea to tape-record the deposition so that you have a real chance to check the accuracy of the deposition. If the opposing attorney objects to your tape-recording it, the attorneys should discuss this before the deposition and come to an agreement.

HOW TO MAKE CHANGES IN YOUR DEPOSITION

If you have made errors during the deposition, you should prevent those errors from being used against you in court. This book describes many factors that can confuse you during the deposition, so changes might be needed. There's a way to make changes in your deposition, as described in the Federal Rules of Civil Procedure. Rule 30(e) states:

"When the testimony is fully transcribed, the deposition shall be submitted to the witness for examination and shall be read to or by him, unless such examination and reading are waived by the witness and by the parties. Any changes in form or substance which the witness desires to make shall be entered upon the deposition by the officer [court reporter] with a statement of the reasons given by the witness for making them. The deposition shall then be signed by the witness, unless the parties by stipulation waive the signing or the witness is ill or cannot be found or refuses to sign."

Note that you don't need a *good* reason to change the deposition transcript. But you must state your reason, whatever it is, and it better be a convincing one. You might say you were tired, confused, or didn't understand the question. However, your reason (e.g., confusion) may not sound good in front of a jury, so be careful of what you say. Make any changes in the deposition transcript with the help of your attorney. According to the rule quoted above, the court reporter makes the changes, but in practice, corrections can be handled in a variety of ways. Changes of importance may lead to another deposition to investigate the new facts.

AVOID AMBIGUOUS "STIPULATIONS"

You may be cheated out of the right to review and correct the deposition transcript. This can occur when stipulations are brought up at the beginning of a deposition. As stated in the American Journal of Trial Advocacy, "Most commonly, the matter of stipulations arises when one attorney asks the question 'The usual stipulations, counsel?' The answer is often an affirmative nod by counsel who, more often than not, is unsure as to the substance of 'the usual stipulations'. . .The end result is that counsel is committed to and bound by 'undefined terms' which may adversely affect the interests of the client. For this reason alone counsel should not agree to. . .blanket stipulations that are inherently ambiguous. If a matter is worth stipulating to, it is worth being specifically set forth in the record by counsel to avoid any ambiguity."

Before your deposition, tell your attorney that you wish to retain the right to review, correct, and sign the deposition transcript. Tell him you wish to be consulted about any stipulations or other agreements that affect the deposition.

PENALTIES IN NOT SIGNING THE DEPOSITION TRANSCRIPT

As we've seen, you can be legally held to your statements in the deposition transcript after you have been cheated out of the opportunity to review and sign it. This shouldn't happen because the patient's attorney should realize that the impeachment value of the transcript is maximized when you sign the document.

Still, if the deposition does remain unsigned, you may be held at the settlement table or in court to statements in the transcript that are inaccurate for various reasons. If you didn't have an opportunity to review the transcript, be sure to bring this up. Judges, juries, and arbitrators may understand that you really didn't have a chance to set the record straight.

Your own delay can destroy your opportunity to review and correct the deposition transcript. Depositions are usually taken with the understanding that there will be a conditional waiver of signature. This means that if the witness doesn't sign the deposition, reasonable opportunity having been given to do so, it may be used with the same force and effect as though it had been read, corrected, and signed.[2]

As stated in the Federal Rules of Civil Procedure, Rule 30(e): "If the deposition is not signed by the witness within 30 days of its submission to him, the officer [court reporter] shall sign it and state on the record the fact of the waiver (or of the illness or absence of the witness or the fact of the refusal to sign together with the reason) . . . and the deposition may then be used fully as though signed unless on a motion to supress. . .."

CONCLUSIONS

Discuss with your attorney the factors concerning the transcription of your deposition. Be familiar with local practices—and your rights. Remember, months, even years, after your deposition, the transcript will always remain to haunt you. Try to make the haunting spirit a friendly one.

The next two chapters discuss the depositions of expert witnesses and other people who can make or break your case. Their depositions will influence yours, and you should influence theirs.

REFERENCES

1. *Malpractice Lifeline.* vol 4, no 4, April 30, 1979.
2. Kornblum GO: Preparation and examination of witnesses, in Davis PA: *Discovery Techniques: A Handbook for Michigan Lawyers.* Ann Arbor, The Institute of Continuing Legal Education, Hutchins Hall, 1977, articles C-3.

3

YOUR EXPERT WITNESSES CAN HELP

The opposition's expert witness helps prepare the deposition questions you will be asked. Your expert witness should help you prepare answers for those questions.

Critical issues in your deposition must be anticipated and discussed with your attorney and expert witness in advance so that you can rehearse important questions before the deposition occurs. Exactly how to rehearse effectively is described in Chapter 12 of this book.

When being sued for malpractice, you will be questioned during your deposition as if you were an expert: You will be asked what references are authoritative, what significance various facts of the case have, and how certain aspects of the treatment affected the outcome. You will be asked hypothetical questions as if you were an expert witness. So it's critical that you understand deposition questioning as it applies to expert witnesses.

Your expert witness can help you to expose the bias and inaccurate statements of opposition witnesses during their depositions by a joint analysis of all deposed material.

THE EXTRA FUNCTIONS OF YOUR EXPERT WITNESS

Medical experts can provide a doctor defendant with many services besides testifying in depositions and in court. When you're being sued, discuss the case in detail with your expert. You'll be able to tell him more about the case than is contained in the medical records. The expert should be able to tell you which aspects of the case are of importance legally.

Be sure that you and your attorney don't withhold information or slant the facts of the case in an attempt to convince your expert that you weren't negligent. The facts will eventually come out. If the expert learns embarrassing information while being deposed by the opposition or while testifying in court, he won't have time to properly consider the information; the results can be disastrous.

Be certain that your medical expert understands and can work with the exhibits of the case. Exhibits can include physical evidence, diagrams, charts, and timetables. The expert should not only be familiar with exhibits, he should help prepare them. If an exhibit is likely to be written on or otherwise distorted, use copies of it during the deposition. If the opposition insists on handling the actual exhibit, have your attorney make it clear the exhibit or evidence is not to be modified in any way. When possible, save the best copy of the real piece of evidence for the settlement table or courtroom.

Your experts can assist in the ways listed in the accompanying table.

BOX 3-1

Functions Of Your Expert Witness In Deposition

> 1. Drafting of written question lists (interrogatories) to be submitted to the opposition.
> 2. Identifying documents in the possession of the opponent or third parties that should be inspected.
> 3. Preparing your attorney to depose (question) the opponent's expert.
> 4. Analyzing depositions that have already been taken.
> 5. Preparing you and others to be deposed.
> 6. Helping prepare diagrams, exhibits, and other information for depositions.

Depending on state law and other circumstances, it may or may not be possible for the plaintiff and defendant to obtain depositions from expert witnesses hired by the other party. The many questioning techniques used to distort the testimony of defendant physicians can also be used against the expert witness.

The opposition's expert is supposed to be unbiased and objective. However, it is unlikely that the patient's attorney will pay an expert to do anything but support the patient's side of the case. So you can expect that an expert has been found who will be of the opinion that you were negligent and are responsible for the damages suffered by the patient.

Reminder: Experts can be intimidated and bought. Some experts are notorious for being "hired guns" who will testify for the right price.

Both sides will find it is desirable to discover, document, and pin down the opposition's expert(s) on many points. Make sure that your side's deposition of the opponent's expert discovers and documents the material in the accompanying table.

BOX 3-2

What Your Attorney Should Discover About The Opposition's Expert

1. Background, including experience with the exact same kind of case being tried.
2. Basis for opinions on the facts of the case.
3. Bias.

There is important information about each of the table's three points that, if pointed out to a jury, may show that the expert isn't to be believed:

1. BACKGROUND: In one recent book, references to cases are given in which it was decided that to be an expert, the physician must have personal knowledge of the subject matter.[1] It is not enough to have read about it. So find out if the expert really has treated patients with the same condition your patient had. If he were managing a case like this, would he call in consultants? What special training has he had in this subject? Has he handled cases with the same complicating circumstances?

Example: When is the last time the witness managed, by himself, a patient like yours: a 65-year-old diabetic with heart and renal failure who gave an unclear history and was on the same chronic medications as your patient? Many professors and other "experts" rarely touch a patient.

Also establish the extent of the expert's expertise. If he's a cardiologist, does he claim to be an expert in pediatric cardiology, invasive cardiology, cardiovascular imaging, exercise physiology, and so on. If he defines his limits of knowledge, this can be brought up when he oversteps his limits. If he isn't an expert in an area relevant to your case, this can be pointed out at an appropriate time.

Through deposition questioning, document the limitations of the opponent's experts. Specifically question them as to whether they have done fellowships in the specialty area involved; if there are people more knowledgeable than they on this subject; whether they have published papers on the question involved; and whether they think that more information about the case would help them come to a more definite opinion. Establish whether or not the expert can imagine any explanation for what happened besides your alleged negligence.

Caution: Don't permit frequent breaks in the middle of the expert's testimony so that he can confer with the patient's attorney. The expert's testimony is supposed to be an unbiased showing of his knowledge. His testimony isn't supposed to be coordinated with the opposition's efforts.

2. BASIS FOR OPINIONS: Document the basis for the expert's opinions. Has he formed them without even examining the patient? Or how much time did he spend with the patient? Does the expert consider any texts to be authoritative? Has he written any? Does the expert's opinion depend on observations the patient made when he was confused or drunk?

If the patient died, it's likely that the expert never did examine the patient. This can be established during the deposition. The courtroom testimony of an expert can be destroyed just by asking the single question, "Doctor, have you ever seen the patient you have told the jury so much about?"

3. BIAS: Does the expert testify often or just for plaintiffs (and not for defendants)? Is the expert being paid for travel, research time, phone calls, hotel bills, consultation time, patient examination time, time spent testifying, time for writing reports, and other items? How much is he getting paid? A long list of payments read at the settlement table or to the jury can document the reason for an expert's bias.

Has the expert gone to the extreme of not keeping written notes of his examination of the patient and other conversations? Some experts are instructed not to keep a written record of their findings for fear that the notes might be examined by the defendant doctor.

Is the expert usually employed by someone? How often does the expert testify for this and other plaintiff's attorneys? Does he have a contingent financial interest in the outcome of the case? (Contingency fees for expert witnesses are illegal.) Is the expert related to or go out socially with the patient, his friends, relatives, or attorney? Has the expert done business with or held stocks in interest of the patient, his attorney, or relatives?

In some personal-injury lawsuits, there are independent experts who haven't been hired by either side. Even when it has been agreed that a witness will be "independent" and therefore more likely unbiased, attorneys may try to "educate" the expert by showing him articles that support one side of the case. Some plaintiff's attorneys will hire the independent expert to do research that will help him see the facts of the case more clearly. Ask any supposedly independent witness if he has done any work or research for the opposition. Such information could document the expert's lack of independence.

Expert witnesses, whether hired by the defense or the plaintiff, can have their testimony impeached (discredited). Don't allow a situation to occur in which the opposition can get information from your expert that will allow statements similar to the following to be made to the jury by the plaintiff's attorney.[2]

"Ladies and gentlemen, I know you don't believe that the physical condition or the right to recover for an injury should be decided as a result of a seven-minute physical examination. The doctor admits he examined 20 people in two hours. That is an average of six minutes per person. Government meat inspectors spend that much time examining a side of beef...For that seven minutes and an hour and a half in this courtroom, he is paid $750. He spent another hour talking to the attorney for the defense interests, but even so, he can't complain about the pay."

SPECIAL SITUATION

During the deposition of a physician witness recently, he was questioned in detail about everything he did in a malpractice case. He'd had a minor part in the case, and there wasn't much to talk about. The care given by the patient's primary physician was the real issue in question. The attorneys asked questions that gave them information that helped them to better understand the case. They could have asked questions more useful to their own purposes if they'd hired an expert to explain the case to them.

The physician witness had been instructed by his attorney to avoid giving any opinions concerning the correctness of the care given by the physician defendant. He wasn't serving as an expert witness. He was simply there to tell what he knew about the case. If asked if he thought the other physician's treatment had been proper, he'd been instructed to simply say, "I have no opinion about that." *This is often the best way to comment on the care given by others.* You'll be asked to explain and defend your answer if you mistakenly say, "I think he did the right thing," or "I don't think he did the right thing." Any answer like that must be supported, defended, and sworn to.

Moral: When asked as a witness about something you didn't actually do or witness, don't feel obligated to answer. Just say, "I have no direct knowledge about that."

CONCLUSIONS

During parts of your deposition you will be questioned as if you were an expert witness. Your expert witness and his deposition can work for or against you, and he can minimize the damage the opposition's expert can do.

The next chapter discusses how the depositions of other witnesses can influence your case and how you should influence those depositions.

REFERENCES

1. Fish RM, Ehrhardt ME, Fish B: *Malpractice: Managing Your Defense.* New Jersey, Medical Economics Books, 1985.
2. Stevenson NC: *Successful Cross-Examination Strategy.* New Jersey, Executive Reports Corporation, 1971.

4

HOW PLAINTIFF'S WITNESSES CAN ENTRAP YOU

Various people may testify in a malpractice deposition, inaccurately describing things you said and did. They may also dishonestly attempt to substantiate claims of disability and pain supposedly suffered by your patient. Such false testimony may trap the unwary physician.

Some legal authorities believe that scarcely a trial is conducted in which perjury doesn't appear. During depositions,the imposing courtroom, judge, and jury aren't present to encourage the deponent to tell the truth. So lies from the opposition during deposition can be expected.

On the other hand, if you're ready for them, the depositions of others can provide information that can be used to your advantage. Any person who knows about a case can be forced to testify in a deposition. These persons include the patient, friends and relatives of the patient, and hospital workers.*This chapter tells how such depositions can make or break your case.* You can greatly help your attorney prepare for his depositions of these other parties.

YOUR FORMER PATIENT IS NOW THE PLAINTIFF

Your former patient can and should be deposed by your attorney. Throughout your deposition and the lawsuit in general, think of your former patient as an adversary, the plaintiff. You're no longer taking care of this person; you're watching out for your own interests. Don't let feelings usually associated with patients soften your attitude toward the plaintiff.

BOX 4-1

If You Believe the Plaintiff Was Wronged

> Suggest to your attorney that a settlement of a certain amount would be appropriate. Watch out for unreasonable claims for pain and suffering, punitive damages, and other impediments to a fair settlement. Whether or not you believe the patient has a valid lawsuit, you're likely to have to fight to limit the amount of damages paid. If not, make a fair settlement and be done with it.

TAKING THE PLAINTIFF'S DEPOSITION

It may be possible to obtain information from the plaintiff that will be helpful at the bargaining table, in court, or in a countersuit. It's important to pin the plaintiff down as to what he or she knows about the case. Especially if he hasn't been coached by his attorney, it may be found that much of the information the plaintiff claimed to have observed was actually learned by talking to others. This would likely be true if the plaintiff were under the influence of alcohol or drugs at the time of treatment. What he "remembers" could actually be what his friends, relatives, or attorney told him.

Claims of damage and issues of liability and contributory negligence can be discovered through depositions of your patient and other persons. In addition to questioning your patient, you will be able to order physical and mental examinations. These examinations are covered in Rules 35(a) and (b) of the Federal Rules of Civil Procedure. Most states have similar rules that allow for the determination of disability and physical and mental condition when such issues are disputed.

It's important to determine if the patient really wants to sue every person named in the lawsuit. If someone has been sued without the patient requesting it, the suit has been brought improperly. The patient's attorney may be liable for damages resulting from suing without cause, as described later in the chapter on countersuits.

The plaintiff, especially if coached by his attorney, will remember aspects of the case favorable to his lawsuit. Facts that might be helpful to you will be forgotten. Only if you let your attorney know in detail what transpired between you and the patient will your attorney be able to demonstrate selective memory loss and untrue statements on the part of the patient.

Make sure your attorney can interpret nurse's notes, medication records, and other obscure aspects of the chart. If the plaintiff exaggerates when describing medication use and complaints of pain, for example, the medical record can be used to discredit his testimony. It might be desirable to do this during his deposition so as to convince him that lies will be detected. Or it might be better to allow him to expand on clearly wrong assertions and collect proof of his lack of character for later use.

When questioning the plaintiff about his disability or other damages, try to define and *limit* the alleged problems.

WEAKENING THE PLAINTIFF'S CLAIMS AGAINST YOU

For example, if informed consent is an issue, the patient can be questioned concerning what he understood about the procedure before it was performed. A series of questions similar to that listed below might bring helpful admissions. Before the plaintiff's deposition, you must tell your attorney what questions you think would be relevant.

- "Did you think the procedure was perfectly safe?"
- "Did you know there was any risk associated with the surgery?"
- "Did you know that all surgery has some risk?"
- "Did you know that you can die or suffer a heart attack when you are put to sleep for any surgical procedure?"
- "Did Dr. Smith guarantee the results of the surgery? Exactly how was this done?"
- "Did you really believe that the results of a surgical procedure could be guaranteed with any certainty?"

The questioning of the plaintiff should bring up difficult medical issues and expose some inconsistencies. This will let the plaintiff know that his claim isn't a sure thing. Educate him to the fact that there are at least two sides to the story and that his testimony is being questioned.

When the plaintiff sees that a battle is ahead and that he may lose everything by going to court, a reasonable settlement may become a possibility. Patients and their families spend a lot of time planning how they're going to spend their settlement money. This is their dream come true, their lottery with one participant. Burst their bubble by showing that they don't have a sure thing.

It's desirable to depose the plaintiff first. He (or she) won't have as much chance to learn about the case from the testimony of other family members and expert witnesses. Because the plaintiff is usually the real "witness" to what happened in a case, it is most desirable to get his observations recorded before they're distorted by the wishful thinking of others.

Concerning the sequence and timing of depositions, Rule 26(d) of the Federal Rules of Civil Procedure states:"Unless the court ... orders otherwise, methods of discovery may be used in any se quence and the fact that a party is conducting discovery, whether by deposition or otherwise, shall not operate to delay any other party's discovery."

COACHING BY THE PLAINTIFF'S ATTORNEY

This can't be prevented before the deposition, but during the deposition it should be kept to a minimum. You are after the truth, not what the plaintiff's attorney wants to be heard.

Tell your attorney to object to frequent coaching. While objections may not stop it, they will document its existence. It's also possible for your attorney to make a statement for the record, stating, for example, that the plaintiff's attorney has interrupted the plaintiff eight times in the last hour, and you have now been waiting three minutes for an answer about which the plaintiff's attorney is coaching his client.

It's also possible to make their conferences inconvenient and embarrassing by having your attorney state during each of their conferences, "Let the record show that the plaintiff is being coached by her attorney," or insist that the conference be on record. The conversation is likely to consist of discoverable material!

WHEN FRIENDS AND RELATIVES OF THE PATIENT BECOME WITNESSES

It is important to ask family members and friends of the plaintiff about what happened, looking for inconsistent statements. Each person may contradict himself from one time to another; statements of different people may conflict. Though many inconsistencies may be minor in nature, a long list of them can severely undercut the witness' credibility at the bargaining table and at trial.[1]

BOX 4-2

Questions To Discover the Basis and Bias of Testimony By the Patient's
Family and Friends

- Do you want to see the patient compensated for his injuries?
- Does the patient owe you money?
- Does the patient live with you?
- How long have you been friends with the patient?
- Do you trust physicians?
- Have you been treated by the defendant physician? What was the result? Did you pay your bills?
- Have you ever been convicted of a felony?
- Were you subpoenaed as a witness, or did you come voluntarily?
- What did the patient's attorney tell you to say?
- Do you have any financial interest in the outcome of this case?
- Did you write any notes about the incident you described soon after it happened?
- Was there a joint session at which several witnesses were prepared to testify? If so, was an effort made to make their statements agree?
- Has anybody helped you refresh your memory concerning what happened?

A plaintiff's friends and relatives may testify about the plaintiff's disability at the trial. You should be able to "discover" what witnesses will be called at trial. These witnesses should definitely be deposed. The Federal Rules of Civil Procedure, Rule 30, states "...After commencement of the action, any party may take the testimony of any person, including a party, by deposition upon oral examination...."

Be sure to document bias, inaccurate memory, and the character of the witnesses. The techniques for exposing inaccurate testimony of such witnesses are the concern of your attorney. However, you may be able to give him suggestions before and during the depositions of these persons if you're familiar with them. Your presence during their depositions will discourage them from exaggerating or lying about you and your treatment of the plaintiff.

During depositions, be prepared to give your suggestions in writing to your attorney. You won't distract him from listening to witnesses, and he will be able to refer to your notes at the proper time.

If you expect someone to be dishonest or prejudiced against you, depose that person early. This prevents the person from learning the testimony in other depositions. The adverse testimony will be more easily impeached (discredited).

The accompanying table lists questions that are especially helpful in assessing the accuracy of testimony given by friends and family. Ask your attorney to raise any of these issues that seem relevant.

TAKING DEPOSITIONS FROM MEDICAL PERSONS

Hospital workers, nurses, and other physicians can be deposed by your attorney. Such witnesses may remember statements you made concerning the case. Attorney Abraham Passman gives an example of a quote that might prove the speaker's negligence:[2]

" ' I shoved the needle into the cartilage, which was very tough, and that caused the needle to break. . .I should have injected it on either side. . .It was my fault she was in the condition that she was-. . .Boy, I sure made a mess of things.' "

If a witness relates that you made similar statements, be able to explain them. The truth is that incompetent physicians don't take time to analyze what happens; they don't learn from experience. It's more likely the competent physician who thinks out loud and discusses cases with colleagues. Competent practitioners are more likely to say, "If I'd used a different technique, the complication wouldn't have occurred." Or, "If I'd given different antibiotics, the patient would be alive today."

Note: Your attorney should remember that such statements aren't evidence of malpractice, as the opposition may claim. In the first example, it may be that the technique used has a lower overall complication rate, but this one complication occurs only with it. In the second example, one might have used the antibiotic that is usually effective for the type of infection being treated, but culture results later showed that another antibiotic would have been better.

Discuss with your attorney how you might effectively explain your statement. If a plaintiff's medical witness quotes a damaging statement you or your attorney may need to give the explanation at your deposition, at the bargaining table, or in court. *Don't volunteer the explanation.* It's best not to show all the defenses that you've prepared.

WHEN THE OPPOSITION CHECKS OUT YOUR MEDICAL WITNESSES

Many plaintiff's attorneys feel it's fair to ask a medical witness about what he remembers before that person's deposition. The witness may meet the plaintiff's attorney for lunch or be called on the telephone.

Example: An operating-room assistant with less than LPN training was present during a procedure that didn't go well. She was phoned a few weeks later and questioned at length about the case.

A malpractice suit was later filed charging the surgeon with negligence in the case. The assistant mentioned to her supervisor that she'd discussed the case at length with someone on the phone, but she didn't know whom she'd spoken to.

BE WARY OF THE OPPOSITION'S MEDICAL WITNESSES

Some people with access to medical records sell information. This probably occurs in many hospitals in the country, though it's rarely found out. In one investigation, evidence was found that hundreds of hospital files were sold to plaintiff's attorneys.[3] Patients were being encouraged to sue their physicians based on information found in illegally obtained charts.

Be especially careful in questioning or deposing nurses and other personnel who dislike any of the defendants. Suspect trouble when one of the physician defendants is the obnoxious type who treats others without respect. People may hold a grudge against him.

If you have medical witnesses give depositions or testify in court to support your case, issue subpoenas for their appearances. If a witness hasn't received a subpoena demanding his appearance, the plaintiff's attorney can claim that the witness came voluntarily. It can be argued that the witness was therefore biased and wanting to help you win your case. Witnesses are supposed to be impartial, and claiming they came voluntarily is one way to "prove" that they're biased.

In general, your medical witnesses who are to testify about what they know of your case don't need to be told about the entire case. They know what they saw and shouldn't be confused or biased by further second-hand information. In contrast, your expert witnesses need to be told everything.

CONCLUSIONS

There are many critical factors in the depositions of plaintiff's witnesses that can affect the outcome of your case. Your former patient and his family members may describe the facts of the case or your treatment inaccurately. Or they may not admit that the patient failed to follow your recommendations. It's your word against theirs. You'll need to tell your attorney what issues to cover so that the truth can be brought out through depositions of the plaintiff, his family and friends, and the opposition's medical witnesses.

The next chapter tells you what information you'll need to gather—dig out—*before* your deposition.

REFERENCES

1. Karlson JN: Special considerations bearing on the depositions of plaintiff's products liability and malpractice actions, in Miller DG: *Taking and Defending Depositions in Personal Injury Cases.* Litigation and Administrative Practice Series, Litigation Course Handbook Series No 236, Practicing Law Institute, pp 163-176.
2. Davis PA: Discovery techniques in malpractice cases, in *Discovery Techniques: A Handbook for Michigan Lawyers.* The Institute for Continuing Legal Education, Hutchins Hall, Ann Arbor, 1977, article C-37.
3. Holoweiko M: The biggest malpractice sellout ever. *Medical Economics,* Feb 18, 1985.

5

GETTING NEEDED INFORMATION
BEFORE YOUR DEPOSITION

Because so many malpractice cases are settled out of court, the only time you may be permitted (or forced) to speak in your defense is during your deposition. Even some attorneys don't understand the importance of preparation for the deposition: "The examination before trial frequently makes or breaks the case...Nevertheless, many trial lawyers who prepare the client rigorously for his or her trial testimony let their associates conduct the client's examination before trial, ofttimes without adequate preparation...One of the little discussed advantages of a well-prepared deposition is the important fact that it greatly facilitates settlement."[1]

Learn the information related to your malpractice lawsuit by (1) studying the facts of your case, (2) attending other malpractice depositions, (3) discussing with your attorney how various problems will be handled with his assistance, and (4) learning about the opposition. Ask your attorney how local laws and customs may affect your deposition.

As one physician-malpractice veteran has said: "You pay a price for being alive today. There are other people on earth who don't have a high degree of ethics. If you don't already know how to deal with them, you'd better lock yourself in a room until you do." (Holoweiko, Mark: Don't let a malpractice suit mess up your mind. Medical Economics, November 26, 1984, pp 62-69.)

That's rhetorical, of course, but the point is that you need to spend many hours, spread over several months, preparing for your deposition. It's like a stage performance in which you're the star player. Preparation is the key element that can save you many thousands or even millions of dollars. It's important to let your attorney know how much effort you're prepared to spend in preparation for your deposition.

Example: One physician surprised his attorney when requesting that he be notified of the depositions of other persons involved in the case. Many physicians don't consider it worth their time to do this. Yet, material discussed in these other depositions is highly relevant to the physician's deposition.

GET INVOLVED

If you find yourself ruminating or worrying about the case in a useless fashion, spend time on constructive activities that will help the case.

And *don't* get involved in certain harmful activities:

1. Avoid speaking or writing to the plaintiff (your former patient) or his attorney. Besides giving them free information, communication with the opposition will void many malpractice insurance policies.
2. Avoid discussing the case with other patients or friends. Patient confidentiality is still a valid excuse for not discussing the case.

Here's the plaintive story of one physician who *didn't* get involved constructively in his malpractice case: " 'I put all my trust in the attorney the insurance company assigned me. . .But in the four years between summons and trial, we met just four times. He didn't prepare me for deposition. . .The plaintiff's charges were so absurd that I wondered how she was going to pay for her legal counsel, expert witnesses, and the distorted anatomical model she'd specially constructed for the occasion.' The doctor found out when the jury awarded the plaintiff more than $1 million.

"Now entangled in his second malpractice suit, the surgeon says: 'This time, I've told my attorney. . .I want to know every detail, and I wouldn't hesitate to speak up if I didn't get it. If need be, I'd ask my malpractice carrier for a replacement. And I'd bring in my own attorney to monitor the case.' "[2]

Even a conscientious defense attorney might not involve the physician as much as he should because he believes the physician doesn't have the time to spend on the case. He may ask for your time only when it's most needed. Your opportunity to help him understand and manage the case at other times will be lost.

Action: Let your attorney know that you want to help him (1) understand the medical records, (2) prepare answers to questions in interrogatories from the opposition, (3) prepare questions to depose the plaintiff with, (4) attend the depositions of others, and (5) work with your expert witness.

KNOW WHAT HAPPENED AND WHEN

"Examining the defendant physician by deposition prior to trial represents the epitome of confrontation between the medical and legal professions. Rarely during medical school, internship, residency or many years of practice is the specialist required to review with such precision the analysis or management of an individual patient."[3]

To help you be familiar with your case, cut up a copy of the chart and put everything in chronological order. If something isn't clearly written, have it typed out. Understand why you might be blamed for a bad result.

A case in point: One malpractice case that illustrates the need for detailed review and knowledge of a case is Mackey v. Greenview Hospital (Mackey v. Greenview Hospital Inc, et al. 587 S.W. 2d 249 Court of Appeals of Kentucky, 1979; Trail WR: Patient's Inaccurate History Loses Case in Legal Aspects of Medical Practice vol 9, no 3, p 7, March 1981). In this case, the patient had denied taking medication or having a heart condition before going to surgery, even though she'd been on a diuretic and nitroglycerin. The surgeon, anesthesiologist, and hospital were sued for malpractice when the patient had a cardiac arrest and suffered brain damage during a breast biopsy.

A nurse had obtained the history of medication before surgery, but this wasn't seen in the patient's chart during surgery. The court found the physicians and hospital not liable because the patient's failure to give a true history was a substantial factor in causing the cardiac arrest. The physicians knew that the nurse's notes weren't available to them at the time of surgery. This detailed knowledge of the case saved them.

Moral: If you believe that something you or anyone else wrote in the chart isn't accurate or that something significant is missing from the charts, define in detail what the truth is. Have a good explanation as to why you believe the entry is inaccurate or missing.

Make up your mind about what is *not* written in the chart. For example, you may not have recorded the fact that you cleansed a wound before suturing it. You're sure that you cleansed it because that is your standard practice. You know for sure, and will state assertively, that you would never suture a wound without cleaning it.

If you claim not to remember some fact during deposition, you may be asked if there are any documents that would refresh your memory. In this way, you're pinned down as to what you do and don't remember. So save time and embarrassment by learning about your case in detail before the deposition.

Check court cases similar to yours. Your attorney can research them. Computerized search services such as Westlaw can be helpful. Westlaw includes an extensive computer record of apellate-court case summaries. The case summaries can be accessed by topic, main words, names, and other means. The service is connected by telephone to computer terminals in libraries and offices.

Other sources of information that may be helpful to your case include federal, state, and local regulations, JCAH standards, and hospital bylaws and regulations.

Study the medical literature relevant to your case. The medical facts as known at the time of your alleged malpractice are relevant. Your treatment won't be judged on the basis of more recent developments, but you may be embarrassed if you don't know about them. If your treatment was shown to be acceptable by articles that came out after you treated your patient, knowledge of this can only help your case. This might occur when you used a drug in an unapproved fashion, but later clinical trials showed the drug would usually be useful in cases similar to yours. Medical books, papers, the Index Medicus, and Med-line are likely to be of help.

What if the literature shows that your treatment wasn't reasonable? A settlement would probably be desirable. For example, a physician's attorney consulted one of us about a case in which an infection led to complications. Medical literature was found showing that inappropriate antibiotics had been used. The attorney chose to ignore this information, went to trial, and lost the case.

YOU'LL NEED DOCUMENTATION OF THE PATIENT'S NON-COMPLIANCE

Physicians often leave information about a patient's continued use of alcohol and other drugs out of the medical records for fear that health insurance won't pay the bills. That's wrong. Since alcohol and drug addiction influence the outcome of many malpractice cases, you'll need chart documentation of your warnings. Your testimony alone may not convince a jury that thinks you're making excuses for the poor result.[4]

Document the failure of the patient to refill prescriptions as often as should have been and to follow up with recommended consultants. The proof of such failures of the patient to comply with your treatment might be available in pharmacy and physician's office records when your malpractice suit is announced. If your patient's non-compliance caused the bad result for which you're being sued, go after such records as soon as you recognize the need for them; if you delay in getting them until late in your suit, they may have been discarded.

The same investigative techniques can be helpful in proving your lack of negligence when it can be shown that a patient had a bad result because of receiving medications from multiple physicians. The fact that a patient who's suing you wasn't taking your medications can also be documented.[5]

When the doctor hasn't explained. Some courts are now claiming that a physician is responsible for the non-compliance of his patient if he failed to explain the possible consequences of the non-compliance. This was the case when a woman who repeatedly refused Pap smears developed fatal cancer. (Truman v. Thomas, 165 Cal Rptr 308, 1980). You'd think that the purpose of Pap smears is common knowledge, but some courts don't seem to think so. When this kind of thing occurs, conscientious physicians make a point of writing in the chart what was told to the patient to explain the dangers of refusing treatment—a big help in any later malpractice suit.

To excuse their own negligence, some people who have seizures, are diabetic, are habitually drunk, or lose consciousness periodically for other reasons sometimes sue their physicians when they have a motor vehicle "accident."[6] If the plaintiff in your malpractice case fits this pattern, before your deposition, research your state's laws. Some states require you to report such people's condition to the state. Even if this were the case, you might not be held responsible for your patient's accident if you discovered that he'd previously been in similar accidents. This can be found by checking his driving record and by questioning at his deposition. One of our patients had over 20 previous traffic citations. The police can check this kind of information.

WHEN OTHER DEFENDANTS ARE INVOLVED

Sometimes your patient will have a bad result because of negligent practices of other physicians, nurses, or the hospital in which care was delivered. It's best to cooperate with other defendants. Plaintiff's attorneys just love it when defendants explain why the other defendants were negligent. Nevertheless, you may at times have to put responsibility where it belongs. Be able to speak about and document your allegations.

Example: One psychiatrist occasionally admitted suicidal patients needing medical treatment to a general medical floor of a hospital because the hospital's psychiatric unit wouldn't take medically unstable patients. Such patients had usually taken overdoses and were often drunk with alcohol in addition to being confused by the medication they'd taken. The psychiatrist was careful to write orders explaining why the drunk and drugged patients were incompetent for purposes of signing out of the hospital against medical advice. When these patients wanted to sign out, the nursing staff let them.

The physician was careful to keep copies of his letters to hospital administration that documented his displeasure with such a practice. These letters would be valuable to the physician if harm befell a patient after leaving the hospital against medical advice. Bringing the matter to committee meetings would also document the physician's concern and lack of control over the situation.

ITEMS TO BE OBTAINED AND STUDIED WHILE PREPARING FOR YOUR DEPOSITION

Following are sources of information that can help your understanding of the case. Plaintiff's attorneys routinely check out such sources.[7] To help you document facts about what occurred, you and your attorney need to do likewise. For example, social service notes may document statements made by the patient concerning his understanding of the treatments offered and indicate how circumstances at home had an adverse effect on his condition after discharge. The person's past work record, available from social service and Internal Revenue Service documents, is of critical importance. This is especially true if the patient claims you've disabled him and must replace his lost future earnings.

Hospital records (often kept in separate files in various places in the hospital): The patient's medical chart; records from peer review committees, pharmacy, X-ray, nursing office, emergency department, laboratory, outpatient department; incident reports; fetal heart-monitoring strips; social service and counseling records; letters to administration; autopsy report; hospital policy and procedure manuals; staff privilege records; consent forms (sometimes on the back of pages in the emergency department chart); notes of interns and residents; medication records; vital sign sheets; fluid balance records; anesthesia and operative reports; recovery room records; discharge summaries.

Your office records: Progress notes; letters to and from referral sources and consultants; letters and forms to and from insurance companies and employers concerning payment, disability, and condition.

Laboratory records: Reports of all radiological examinations and laboratory tests. If you can't get original X-rays, they should be studied and copies obtained.

Information documenting the patient's condition before and after your treatment: Records from hospitalizations; employment; state department of motor vehicles; insurance companies; and the military.

Other sources: Ambulance and police records documenting condition and degree of cooperation; pharmacy records documenting medicines taken; physical therapy records documenting condition and treatment; medical records from other hospitals and physicians; investigation documenting employment, drug and alcohol use, criminal record, previous lawsuits, insurance claims, previous hospitalizations; coroner's report.

You and your attorney need to be wary when interpreting the records and other information you check out. For example, clauses in consent forms that relieve the physician of the duty to exercise reasonable care or that waive the right of the patient to make claims for negligent care will usually be held as *invalid.* You can't sign away the right to expect competent care.[8]

Investigating the facts can pay off. In one case, a physician urged his attorney to settle a case before the facts of the case were investigated. An obese woman, who'd received an injection in her buttock, complained of pain there. An X-ray showed half an inch of broken needle in the area. The woman sued the physician for $50,000, though his nurse denied the needle had broken.

Investigation showed that the X-ray image was that of a sewing needle rather than of a hypodermic needle. The woman had worked for a short time as a seamstress.

Moral: Settlement wasn't necessary in that case. Don't let anyone needle you into a settlement, or even a deposition, until you've investigated the facts of your malpractice case.

YOUR ATTORNEY NEEDS TO KNOW WHEN YOU'RE AT FAULT

There may be some embarrassing facts about your case. Perhaps you did tell your patient to get lost because he didn't pay his bills. Or maybe you modified the medical record. Your attorney will be better able to help you map out your deposition strategy if he knows all the facts.

You may be afraid that some fact will invalidate your insurance, especially if it proves to be fraudulent or criminal acts on your part. If so, you may want to consult another attorney before you go to the one hired by your insurance carrier.

CASE NO. 1: One physician did tell his attorney the truth about altered records. His signed medical record indicated that a baby had been in an Isolette with extra oxygen. After learning of a lawsuit for allegedly causing retrolental fibroplasia (sometimes linked to excess oxygen), the physician carefully read the note he'd signed saying that extra oxygen had been given. In fact, extra oxygen hadn't been given, but the physician signed the note without carefully reading it.

Later when the lawsuit was announced, the physician crossed out the word "with" and wrote "without." A copy of the chart had previously been sent to the state Medicaid agency and was readily available. The physician's attorney was told of the change of records and let the opposition know about it. An open admission was made, and the suit brought the plaintiff much less than had been asked for. Honesty paid off.

CASE NO. 2: Another physician didn't level with his attorney. The physician claimed that notes written in smaller handwriting on one part of his chart were made within hours of when the patient left his office. However, a photocopy of the chart (without the added sections) was produced by the opposition at the last minute: during trial. The physician had to invoke the Fifth Amendment 25 times and was advised to hire a criminal lawyer because he'd perjured himself both in his deposition and in court. The settlement was large.[9]

CONCLUSIONS

Get involved with your case long before the depositions start. Study the appropriate medical literature, get all the records involved in the case, and don't let anyone needle you into a settlement.

The next chapter deals with the specific kinds of help your attorney can give you in your deposition.

REFERENCES

1. Agoglia EJ: Some general principles in preparing personal injury clients for deposition, in Miller DG: *Taking and Defending Depositions in Personal Injury Cases.* Practicing Law Institute Litigation and Administrative Practice Series, Litigation Course Handbook Series No 236, 1983.

2. Holoweiko M: Don't let a malpractice suit mess up your mind. *Medical Economics* 1984, Nov 26.

3. Werchick A: Deposing the doctor defendant, in Miller DG: *Taking and Defending Depositions in Personal Injury Cases.* Practicing Law Institute Litigation and Administrative Practice Series, Litigation Course Handbook Series No 236.

4. Carlova J: Cut your malpractice risk in half. *Medical Economics* 1984, Dec 24.

5. Gregory DR: *Criminal involuntary manslaughter.* Legal Aspects of Medical Practice, vol 10, no 3, March, 1982.

6. Marco CH: *Liable for epileptic driver?* Legal Aspects of Medical Practice, vol 11, no 7, July, 1983.

7. Weitz H: Predisposition discovery in malpractice actions, in Miller DG: *Taking and Defending Depositions in Personal Injury Cases.* Practicing Law Institute Litigation and Administrative Practice Series, Litigation Course Handbook Series No 236, Aug 29, 1983, pp 73-89.

8. Gregory DR: *Duty to reasonable care voids exculpatory clause.* Legal Aspects of Medical Practice, vol 10, no 4, April, 1982.

9. Boronson W: Would your malpractice defense really hold up? *Medical Economics* 1985, May 27.

6

WORKING WITH YOUR ATTORNEY
BEFORE AND DURING DEPOSITION

Under the law, you can't do much in depositions besides answer questions. You can't refuse to answer questions unless so instructed by your attorney. By yourself, you can't ask questions of the plaintiff's attorney or object to unreasonable questions. By yourself, you're powerless in many situations.

That's why you need every bit of help you can get from your attorney in handling difficult, upsetting, unfair, and confusing situations. You must work closely with him before—and during—deposition to make the cooperative effort successful.

For one thing, you must learn the opposing attorney's methods. Analyze those methods and discuss them with your attorney. Have him try to obtain copies of depositions the plaintiff's attorney has participated in. He may be able to get these from other physicians or your malpractice insurance company.

Whether or not your attorney can obtain previous depositions involving the opposing attorney, impress on your attorney that you want full protection against unreasonable treatment. Tell him you expect him to object if opposition questions ask for privileged information. You expect him to object if questions are argumentative, unreasonably repetitive, ambiguous, complex, or otherwise open to misinterpretation.

MOST QUESTIONS FROM THE OPPOSITION
ARE TRAPS

You'll be able to answer many questions yourself. Some, however, will require objections or requests for clarification. You're not required to answer questions that are unclear or ambiguous. Before your deposition, discuss with your attorney how you would jointly handle such questions and various other situations. He should be the one to:

- Make objections to questions.
- Ask that a recess be held when you're looking tired.
- Complain about intimidating opposition behavior.
- Demand that distracting spectators leave.
- Insist that there not be smoking in the room (if you're a non-smoker).
- Stop any disrespectful treatment that you receive.

Go over with your attorney the types of unreasonable questions that appear later in this chapter. Discuss how *he* would deal with these various situations. Discuss how you can let him know during the deposition that you want him to intervene.

In general, he should do all he can to counter unreasonable questions and treatment before you do say anything (aside from calling his attention to the problem).

Once your attorney has done all he can, you must continue where he left off. For example:

Plaintiff's attorney: Doctor, do you not remember Mr. Jones telling you he had not had chest pain exactly like this before and that he was a diabetic?

Physician's attorney: Please, one clear question at a time.

Plaintiff's attorney: The doctor is intelligent enough to answer a simple question. I object to your repeated interruptions.

Physician (taking his attorney's hint): I did not catch your first question. Please repeat it.

Plaintiff's attorney: Do you not remember Mr. Jones telling you he had not had chest pain exactly like this before?

Physician: Your question is not clear. Please rephrase it.

Plaintiff's attorney: Did Mr. Jones tell you he had had chest pain exactly like this before?

If prearranged signals don't convey enough meaning, whisper to your attorney during the deposition when something is bothering you. If this isn't possible, ask that you be allowed to take a recess to confer with him. When asked why this is necessary, you may say, "Because you have been harrassing and badgering me." During the recess tell your attorney what you want, such as objections to questions, respectful treatment, newspaper reporters out of the room, or a seat further from the plaintiff's attorney.

WHEN YOUR ATTORNEY DOESN'T PRODUCE

Your attorney may not want to put the needed effort into watching out for all your interests. He may be concerned about getting through the deposition quickly because there's a bigger case he must prepare, or perhaps it is his wife's birthday. Or he may just be lazy. Whatever the reason, don't tolerate anything short of maximum effort. He's being paid for his work.

He may be intimidated by the plaintiff's attorney: Some lawyers are masters of intimidation and bluffing. Your attorney may complain about unreasonable questions and unfair treatment you receive during deposition and be told he's crazy to complain. If the plaintiff's attorney is well-known or more experienced than your attorney, your attorney may think there's nothing that can be done. He must demand your rights for you; you're powerless by yourself in this matter. Don't be bullied!

He wants to facilitate a settlement: That's another reason your attorney may want to avoid confrontation and friction in your deposition. Probably for this reason, the tone of conversation and demeanor of attorneys during depositions is often one of friendliness. Sometimes it's hard to believe there's a legal battle going on. Be courteous, but don't give up your rights or self-respect to avoid disagreement. No matter how nice you are, the plaintiff's attorney is going to try to get all the money he can from you. Sooner or later, the facade of friendliness is usually dropped.

Once it's dropped, questioning can get tough. If you find your attorney being insensitive to rough treatment you're receiving, it may be that he sees such treatment frequently and thinks nothing of it. But take him aside, tell him what's bothering you, and discuss what he might do about it.

CAN ANOTHER ATTORNEY HELP?

If your attorney doesn't cooperate fully with you, consider asking your insurance company to appoint another attorney to the case. Insurance companies often assign malpractice cases to local law firms, so you might be able to have an entirely different firm represent you. Speak to other physicians in your area to learn about the firms that might possibly represent you.

One physician in our area called his insurance carrier when he heard that he was being sued. He requested that the hospitals attorney not represent him because he was familiar with the man's unacceptable work. The physician's carrier accepted the free advice.

If you plan to complain to your carrier about their attorney, document the problems you've been having. Have copies of letters showing that the attorney hasn't agreed to meet to help you with deposition questions you expect to be asked, hasn't investigated the background of the opposition's witnesses, or whatever the case may be.

WHEN TO HIRE YOUR OWN ATTORNEY

1. You'll want to hire your own attorney to work with the carrier's attorney if the claim exceeds your coverage. Your attorney should help you avoid settling for an amount that exceeds your coverage. He should also make sure that the defense strategy addresses the full amount of the claim.[1]

2. You'll also need your own attorney if your insurance carrier says it won't cover you. There are a variety of reasons why carriers refuse to accept responsibility for malpractice cases. These reasons depend on the insurance contract and may include: the physician being sued as a supervisor rather than as a physician; a physician being sued because he is a partner of a supposedly negligent physician; or the physician didn't notify the company immediately when there was a hint that the suit might come up in the future.

3. You'll need your own separate attorney if you disagree with your carrier when it comes time to settle. The carrier's attorney is being paid by the carrier and may not have your interests at heart. In such cases, you might want to hire a separate attorney. Some insurance companies see settlements only in terms of money: If it costs less to settle than it would to continue defending the case, the case will be settled. Other carriers feel that the settlement of nuisance suits will encourage attorneys to file more lawsuits than is justified. They hesitate to settle non-meritorious cases.

Many physicians feel that their reputations are on the line when they're sued. They feel it's a matter of principle when a suit is settled. So if you don't see eye-to-eye with your carrier on settlements, you may need to hire another attorney—or maybe even countersue.

Example: In one case, a surgeon sued the attorneys who had been retained by his insurance company to defend a charge of malpractice against him. The physician claimed that the attorneys settled the case without his permission and knowledge. He claimed that in his deposition he proved that there was no negligence on his part.

Despite that fact and physician's instructions to the insurance company's attorneys not to settle, a settlement was negotiated. Under the terms of the malpractice insurance policy, the company was authorized to settle without the physician's consent. The appellate court found, however, that when the insurer's attorneys became aware that a settlement was imminent and that the physician didn't want the case settled, a conflict arose that prevented their continuing to represent both the physician and the insurance company.

The court found that the attorneys had a duty to act as if the physician had hired them directly. When the conflict arose, they should have informed both the physician and the insurance company of the problem (Rogers v. Robson, Masters, Ryan, Brumund, and Belom Ill., 407 N.E. 2d 47). You can't count on your court following the precedent of this Illinois case. Settle conflicts or hire another attorney before a final out-of-court settlement or other unacceptable action takes place.

4. You may need your own attorney if you feel that your carrier's attorney doesn't trust you. He may have a general lack of trust in doctors. He may seem to assume you were negligent before examining the facts of the case. He may drag his feet while investigating the case, try to push you into a settlement, won't let you examine documents, or won't take your suggestions concerning questions to use while deposing the plaintiff and his family.

Your carrier's attorney may not be adequate because of lack of experience in malpractice cases. Malpractice is a specialized area of law. Accept only an attorney who has had experience in malpractice cases—preferably as a junior partner in a law firm. Meet with your attorney frequently enough to make sure he's performing the tasks described in this chapter.

Example: One of us consulted on a malpractice case two months before trial. The physician's attorney wasn't familiar with the usual treatment or outcome of cases similar to that being considered. His knowledge of anatomy left much to be desired. He didn't seem too interested when we gave him articles that explained the information he lacked. He didn't ask any questions.

In conferences held to discuss the case with the attorney, the defendant physician was noticeably absent. The physician and his attorney thought the claims of the patient were exaggerated, which indeed they were.

The jury didn't think so. The physician lost the case, partly because his attorney didn't understand the medical facts of the case, and partly because the physician did a poor job of answering questions about the case.

In contrast, another defense attorney in a malpractice case in the same town collected information about the opposing attorney and tall stacks of depositions that had been given in various cases by the opposition's expert witness. These were available for study long before the first deposition was taken. The defendant doctor won the case.

Moral: Judge the performance of your carrier's attorney. If he falters, ask him about it. If you're not satisfied, consider getting another attorney.

Reminder: Attend opposition depositions in your case. At the very least, have your attorney tell you what transpired during each deposition. In any event, read the transcripts at your leisure. Another reason to attend depositions is that plaintiffs and their relatives are less likely to lie about what happened if you're staring them in the face!

YOUR ATTORNEY CAN HELP YOU REHEARSE

You can also practice with a videotape recorder on your own, paying special attention to facial expressions and body language. Ask your partner or doctor friends to insult and trick you, using the techniques described later in this book.

Don't memorize pat answers to questions: It's impossible to anticipate the variety of questions you'll be asked. So ask your attorney to take you through a serious questioning session under simulated deposition conditions. The environment shouldn't be unrealistically comfortable; there should be no drinks or interruptions. An attorney unfamiliar to you might be present to question or bother you. Questions are likely to be difficult. You'll get real combat training. After that deposition, review the conversation with your attorney.

During your real deposition realize that certain claims on your part can be expected to lead to related questions. Don't open new avenues of discovery unless you are ready to enter them. For example, you may state, "No matter how skilled the surgeon and what pecautions are taken, ten percent of patients undergoing this procedure die, just as my patient did."

After such a statement, you can expect (and should have answers prepared for) the following series of questions:

"Where do those statistics come from?"
"What scientific controls were used in that study?"
"Did other studies confirm those results?"
"Would a bad result be more likely if the surgeon were less skilled?"
"What circumstances made this patient fall within the category of patients referred to in the studies?"

In addition to questions you inadvertently suggest to the opposition, there are hundreds of standard questions that plaintiff's attorneys ask. Many of these are listed in the tables that follow. Practice answering them with your attorney, preferably in front of a video camera.

Some questions are listed together as they might actually be asked in a deposition. Answer them in order, with your attorney, one at a time. Other potential opposition questions listed are vague or objectionable for other reasons—and thus well worth rehearsing.

Think of how you would say that the question isn't clear. Keep these questions in mind as you read later chapters, and come back to practice them. If you don't know how you would answer any of them, discuss them with your attorney *before* your deposition! There are four main categories:[2]

COMMON DEPOSITION QUESTIONS

Questions About You
- What is your full name and office address?
- Where were your previous practice addresses?
- In what states are you licensed?
- When and how did you become licensed?
- When and from what medical school did you graduate?
- Where did you do your internship and residency? What were the dates? Did you successfully complete the training?
- What, if any, specialty do you practice?
- Are you board-certified or qualified in any specialties?
- When and how did you become board-certified? Did you fail any part of the examination the first time? Why?

- What ailments or conditions does your specialty deal with?
- To what medical societies and professional associations do you belong?
- What must be done to become a member of these organizations? What offices, elected or appointed, have you held? To what committees have you belonged? Have you published or contributed to any medical publications? Were the publications based on research you performed? Describe the research and its results.
- What research do you have in progress? How much of your time does it take? How much are you compensated for it?
- What hospitals and medical schools are you affiliated with?

Questions About Your Care

- How did it happen that you came to treat this patient?
- What do you remember about this case without reference to the records? Do you really recall the details? Which ones?
- What was the patient's appearance?
- Relate the history you took from him that helped you in making your diagnosis. What questions did you ask? Were they all answered? Did you record all pertinent positives and negatives, or are some findings assumed normal because they're not recorded in the medical record?
- Did you note subjective symptoms and objective signs related to the patient's condition in the chart?
- What were they?
- What physical examinations and laboratory tests were performed in the course of your examination?
- What were the findings of your examinations?
- What was your differential diagnosis at this point? What possibilities seemed most likely?
- Were X-rays taken? Where were they taken? How many X-rays and what views were taken?
- Were the X-rays examined by a radiologist? When? Did you depend upon the radiologist's interpretation of the X-rays? Did you agree with his interpretation?
- What consultations, if any, were called? Did you follow their advice? Why or why not? Do you usually ask for consultations in such cases?
- On what did you base your diagnosis?
- Did you have any reason to doubt your diagnosis?
- What treatment was prescribed?
- What is your opinion concerning the nurse's notes that stated the patient continued to have pain despite your treatment?

- Did the treatment work?
- Why did you select the treatment given?
- Did you see any reason to change your diagnosis or differential diagnosis at a later time? If so, indicate when and why you made your new diagnosis. What actions did you take as a result?
- How often do you get the complication which occurred?
- What determines whether this complication can be expected?
- How do your statistics compare to those of other surgeons?
- What precaution could have prevented the complication?
- In your opinion, was it a departure from accepted medical practice not to have taken more X-rays?
- Was the patient cooperative with the treatment?
- Did the patient cause or contribute to the poor outcome?
- Does the PDR®list contraindications of the drugs you used that would make them inappropriate in this case?
- What medically recognizable factors could possibly explain the events in dispute?
- Was any other person negligent in the care of this patient?
- Did you continue to treat and examine the patient?
- Identify and describe all blood vessels that lead from the area of interest. Further describe the anatomy of the region of interest. Were the nerves and blood vessels identified? How, and by whom?
- Is it not a surgical error to incise the nerve that was damaged?
- What steps did you take to remedy this irregularity?
- Isn't it a fact that severing that nerve will lead to permanent paralysis?

Establishing Damages and Liability
- Will you state the name of each person who assisted in or witnessed the care of the patient?
- Did you observe or were you ever informed that any person assisting in the care of the plaintiff was inefficient or negligent in the performance of his or her duties at the time? Please describe the irregularity.
- What anesthesia was administered to the patient? Was it local or general? Who administered the anesthesia? Did he or she remain with the patient throughout the operation?
- Who supervised the person administering the anesthesia? What was the nature of the immediate supervision?
- When did you last examine the patient?
- What is the current mental and physical condition of the patient?

- What is the prognosis of the patient?
- At the time you treated the patient, were you the member of a partnership or professional corporation? What was its nature?
- What past partnerships have you belonged to? What physicians were members of those partnerships?

The Big Traps

- In preparation for this deposition, what documents did you review, including records, books, notes, bills, depositions of others, X-rays, and journals?
- Whom did you speak to in preparation for this deposition? What was the content of your conversations? Did you make an effort to have your statements agree with those of your colleagues?
- Has this case been the subject of correspondance, article, formal lecture, or discussion with other physicians? Please describe them.
- What are the titles and authors of the last three journal article you have read?
- Is your memory clear about these events?
- Are you certain about that?
- What publications do you own or subscribe to that discuss this subject? These are authoritative, are they not? Why do you subscribe to them?
- Did the patient suffer any complications from your medical treatment? If so, what are your explanations for the complications? Are the complications normally anticipated with this type of procedure?
- Was the possibility of this complication explained to the plaintiff prior to the procedure? Was he able to understand the explanation? How do you know; he was medicated, was he not?
- Do your hospital bylaws require you to record information in the medical record that you omitted? When were your chart entries written and dictated? Why was there a delay?
- What recent meetings have you attended that covered the kind of case your patient had? Why did you feel the need to attend these meetings?
- Name each prior deposition examination you have attended. Were you a defendant, witness, or expert? What were the medical issues? What was the result of your depositions?
- Have you ever been disciplined, had your license revoked, or had your hospital privileges limited or revoked?
- Have you ever been reprimanded, censured, punished, or suspended from practice by any society or institution?

- Have you ever been accused of malpractice, misfeasance, or malfeasance? If so, describe the incidents, their dates, and their results.
- In what hospitals do you currently have privileges? Have you ever had an application for privileges rejected?
- Do you teach? What subjects? How many hours a week do you teach? What is your compensation?
- What insurance coverage do you have for this event? What is your insurance carrier; dollar amounts; limitations on coverage applicable to this case?
- Have you ever been denied insurance coverage of any kind? Why?
- What lawsuits have been filed against you in the past?
- Do you have a criminal record?
- Do you consider any texts authoritative?
- What texts were used in your training?

YOUR ATTORNEY CAN HELP YOU KNOW THE ENEMY

Find out about the plaintiff and the attorney who are suing you, and about the patient's family. Questioning the plaintiff, of course, can pin him down as to what he knows and remembers about the case. You and your attorney can use depositions to learn about the character and ability of the plaintiff to handle questioning by the opposition.

Find out about the plaintiff's relatives. They may still be your patients. It wouldn't be surprising if you felt like dismissing the plaintiff's entire family from your practice. Malpractice attorney Jack E. Horsley of Mattoon, Illinois, argues, however, that if the offending patient or a family member keeps coming to you for treatment—as often happens—you should consider it ammunition for trial. "The jury will wonder how bad a doctor you could be if those who sued still value your services," says Horsley.[3]

Ask attorneys who know the patient's attorney about him. These sources of information must be sophisticated, sympathetic to your cause, and honest.

Example: One physician was being sued by an attorney we'll refer to as Mr. Smith. The physician asked an assistant state's attorney about Smith. The attorney had worked in town only a few years and was just starting his career. He said that Smith was a fair, reasonable person with a good reputation. On the other hand, several other lawyers in town related that Smith was an irrational alcoholic. He took cases with no merit and harrassed witnesses in a way that made other attorneys apologize for him.

A legal directory can provide information about the opposing attorney, including his or her education. A computerized legal research service can provide references to the attorney's past cases. Review the cases to find out about the attorney's honesty, previous performance, and usual tactics. Obtain information about the attorney's willingness to settle.

CONCLUSIONS

You must depend on your attorney to help you through your ordeal. And you need to be familiar with the many standard malpractice-deposition questions that are part of the plaintiff's attorney's arsenal.

The next chapter deals with time pressures, a potentially frustrating problem you'll encounter before and during your deposition.

REFERENCES

1. Westcott CE: Six signs that you need to hire your own lawyer, *Medical Economic* 1983, June 13.
2. Deposition questions are drawn from (1) Davis PA: *Discovery Techniques: A Handbook for Michigan Lawyers.* 1977, Library of Congress catalog card No 77-88850. The Institute of Continuing Legal Education, Hutchins Hall, Ann Arbor, Michigan; (2) Werchick A: Deposing the doctor defendant, pp 91-108 in Miller DG:*Taking and Defending Depositions in Personal Injury Cases.* Practicing Law Institute; (3) Haydock and Herr, 1982; (4) Shandell, 1981; and (5) Dolan JE: *Examination Before Trial and Other Disclosure Devices.* Acme Law Book Company, Amityville, NY, 1974 (and 1975 supplement).
3. Holoweiko M: Don't let a malpractice suit mess up your mind, *Medical Economics* 1984, Nov. 26.

7

DON'T LET TIME PRESURES
GET YOU DOWN

Lost time and inconveniences before and during malpractice depositions frequently make physicians tired, frustrated, and angry. As a
result, they lose the desire and ability to defend their interests in depositions. A common complaint of defense attorneys is that they
can't get physicians to cooperate with their own defense. These doctors don't realize that a relatively small amount of time properly
spent before and during a deposition will minimize the damage the
deposition can do.

Time pressures are an unavoidable part of the legal process,
though some plaintiff's attorneys deliberately make things worse
than they need be. As we'll see, they use such tactics as delaying the
lawsuit for years, changing the times of meetings, making depositions too long, and asking unfair questions.

When some physicians give a deposition, they're more interested in getting back to the office quickly than in giving proper answers.
They're fed up with the case. Patient's attorneys know of the reluc-
tance of physicians to spend time on legal matters, and some attorneys capitalize on the physician's failure to assist with his defense.

Yet a relatively small amount of time properly spent on certain
tasks can help your case significantly. The deposition, like the entire
lawsuit, is a kind of waiting game. If you grow impatient and lose
your temper, you'll make statements that will hurt your case. If you
simplify answers in an attempt to shorten the deposition, you'll
make inaccurate, damaging statements.

REALIZE THAT ANSWERING QUESTIONS PROPERLY MAY TAKE LONGER

It may take, say, ten hours more than you might expect to deal effectively with the opposition in a deposition. But $100,000 might be saved. That's $10,000 an hour. And that doesn't include the savings to your reputation, conscience, and self-esteem.

As long as you're providing information or becoming frustrated, the opposition's purposes are being served. If you're calm and the opposition isn't getting any special information, no harm is being done to you.

The plaintiff's attorney may make you try to answer quickly or simplify your answers. He may become indignant if you ask for a minute to consider your answer. If he or other witnesses become impatient, don't feel sorry for them. Face it: If they'd limit their activities to a straightforward discussion of the case at hand, the deposition would end quickly. They're there to sue you; if they're frustrated with the progress or can't stay long enough to finish the job, it's to your advantage.

Moral: Recognize deliberately caused time pressures for what they are.

WHY SHOULD YOU SPEND TIME DEFENDING A MALPRACTICE CASE?

There are several reasons. Many cases with minor damages have been blown out of proportion, leading to awards of hundreds of thousands of dollars. Each such case raises insurance premiums for all physicians and encourages patients and lawyers to sue even more than they already are doing. Also, if the amount awarded to the patient is greater than your policy will pay, or if your policy doesn't pay for some technical reason, the award will come out of your pocket.

Even if it isn't justified from a medical viewpoint, lawyers will go after your money. They are taught to do just that.[1] "We were introduced to the concept of the the 'deep pocket'—that's an individual with a bank account healthy enough to make it worth an attorney's time to go after him for damages of one variety or another. . .Even in hypothetical cases having nothing to do with medical negligence—say, a four-car pileup on an interstate—instructors would point out that an M.D. license plate was a sure signal that this was your bird to soak."

Remember your status as a bird that can be soaked when dealing with attorneys.

RECOGNIZE THE DIFFERENCE BETWEEN TIME WASTED AND TIME WELL SPENT

Chances are that the greatest amount of time you spend on your case will be spent worrying about the case; a threat that hangs over one's head for years is a burden. Non-productive conversations with your spouse and colleagues will also consume significant amounts of time. This constant rumination and unproductive worry can lead to depression, ineffectiveness in your medical practice, and even (as has happened to some physicians) suicidal thoughts.

Instead of letting your medical practice slide, make a special effort to be more thorough with each case, more courteous to each patient, and more rigorous in your record keeping. If you feel persecuted or picked on, try reading about the history of various religions or other literature that deals with human nature. If you feel you must do something to help your case, read the works of the plastic surgeon Maxwell Maltz. Some of his ideas are presented in Chapter 13 of this book.

Reminder: The deposition and trial are when effective action is needed. Since most malpractice cases are settled without going to trial, preparing for and doing well at the deposition is probably the only effective way to spend your time.

Here's how plaintiff's attorneys use time pressures to your disadvantage.

DELAYING ACTIONS UNTIL THE LAST POSSIBLE MOMENT

The statute of limitations allows two or more years, depending on the state and the circumstances, for a malpractice suit to be filed. It's not unusual for a suit to be filed within days of the deadline. Such delays make it difficult for the physician to remember details of the case. Original X-rays may have been put on lesser-quality microfilm. Colleagues who remember the case may have moved away.

While many of us can maintain a fighting spirit for a few months, after a few years, we're just sick and tired of the lawsuit. Knowing that the opposition is hoping you lose interest in the lawsuit should motivate you to act effectively when needed. Still, you should put the lawsuit out of your mind when there is little you can do but wait.

CHANGING THE TIME OF APPOINTMENTS

Depositions are often cancelled and rescheduled by the plaintiff's attorney: He was called to court on another case. Something important came up. A judge wanted a conference about another case. The jury in another case the plaintiff's attorney is involved with can't come to a decision in a trial that should have ended last week. And so on. So your appointment is rescheduled.

Physicians, on the other hand, are expected to keep appointments, get other physicians to care for their patients, and cancel office hours.

There are several things you can do to help your interests when appointments, including depositions, are cancelled. Use the unexpected free time to do something you've been wanting to do. And don't get angry: A certain amount of schedule-changing is normal and unavoidable. But if an unreasonable number of appointments are cancelled at the last minute, it's likely to be a ploy to frustrate you and weaken your resolve.

Tip: Obtain written evidence that appointments were made, and document the cancellations by writing letters to your attorney about them. Proof of repeated cancellation of meetings may later help you prove that the opposing attorney had malicious intent in bringing the suit. Some types of countersuits must show malicious intent, so this evidence can be important. Even if you don't later file a countersuit, you can submit bills (and may be able to sue) for your time lost at work.

The following quote by a physician defendant from a malpractice deposition illustrates the kind of relentless appointment-cancelling some physicians have faced:

"I want my statement recorded in this deposition transcript. When this deposition was first scheduled on January 9th, I was the only one who showed up. Then, on January 21st when you knew I would be on vacation, you scheduled a hearing with the judge that I could not attend. The deposition was next scheduled on February 5th in the afternoon. I was called that morning and told that it was being cancelled. I had already cancelled all my appointments for that afternoon.

The deposition was next scheduled for March 3rd. I was called the day before and told that Mr. Smith was sick. Again, I lost half a day of work. The deposition was rescheduled for April 4th. Two days before that I was called and told that Mr. Jones would be in court. The deposition was set and cancelled twice more."

That kind of appointment-cancelling can put a plaintiff's attorney at jeopardy. The Federal Rules of Civil Procedure deal with the failure to attend depositions in Rule 30(g)(1): "If the party giving the notice of the taking of a deposition fails to attend and proceed therewith and another party attends in person or by attorney in pursuant to the notice, the court may order the party giving notice to pay such other party the reasonable expenses incurred by him and his attorney in attending, including reasonable attorney's fees."

ADDING HOURS TO THE DEPOSITION BY ASKING IMPROPER QUESTIONS

We'll talk about how to deal with improper questions later in this book. Though there are ways you can deal with them, your first line of defense is your attorney. If he doesn't object to unreasonable questions, take a short break and ask him to explain why.

Some questions are improper because they deal with information the opposition has no right to know. These would include those about irrelevant or privileged information. Other questions are improper because they can trick you into giving untrue answers. Examples are those which are leading, multiple, or complex. You can also be led astray by hypothetical questions and questions containing words with multiple or emotional-laden meanings.

Another category of question you won't enjoy answering is the repetitive question. Some amount of repetition is unavoidable because it's reasonable to approach a subject from several different angles. However, physicians and nurses are often subjected to hours of repetitious testimony during depositions.

If one deposition seems bad to you, try five. A nurse we know was forced to testify at depositions called by the plaintiff, the two defendant physicians, and the two hospitals that employed the physicians. The nurse describes her fifth deposition: "They kept trying to get me to say that Dr. Jones had ordered the wrong medication. I'd told them so many times what happened, but they just kept asking. They would go off on another subject for a while, then come straight back to that same question. They must have asked me about that one point a dozen times. Every once in a while when I'd finished speaking, four lawyers would start to write on their papers; you would think they had it all down by now. They were trying to upset me."

The asking of repetitious questions is a form of badgering. Intimidating behavior, such as raising the voice and approaching you in a threatening manner, may accompany badgering. Such behavior is allowed to a certain extent because it will bring the truth out of some people. However, badgering and intimidation can cause other people to become so nervous they don't know what they're saying. In court, the judge will determine if badgering and intimidation have gone too far. In a deposition, the judge isn't present, so your attorney must object to unreasonable treatment, or at least make sure it's documented in the deposition transcript.

Caution: If the opposition really does give you a hard time, remember that the deposition transcript is a legal document. Don't behave improperly yourself. The deposition transcript will be useful if you later want to file a countersuit.

WASTING TIME FOR NO REASON

As stated in a recent issue of the American Bar Association Journal, "Depositions expand to meet the time allotted for them. If the truth of this does not immediately conjure up images of dozens of depositions you've attended, then you've been lucky. If the issues are simple, you are well organized, and you get the testimony you want in two hours in a deposition scheduled for two days, why waste everybody's time fishing around?"[2]

CONTINUING THE DEPOSITION

If you don't finish the deposition in one day, you'll be required to come back another day. This may be done because not all items have been covered or because someone in the deposition was called away or became ill.

Another reason depositions are continued is that the opposition wants to gather more information, take depositions from others, and then question you in the light of what has been learned in the meantime. Before your deposition, ask your attorney if the local laws can prevent or make it difficult for the opposition to order you back for another grilling.

Federal law now requires that depositions not be unreasonably duplicative, burdensome, or expensive. It's spelled out in the Federal Rules of Civil Procedure. Rule 26(b)(1) states in part: "The frequency or extent of use of the discovery methods. . .shall be limited by the court if it determines that: (i) the discovery sought is unreasonably

Malpractice Depositions

cumulative or duplicative, or is obtainable from some other source that is more convenient, less burdensome, or less expensive; (ii) the party seeking discovery has had ample opportunity by discovery in the action to obtain the information sought; or (iii) the discovery is unduly burdensome or expensive, taking into account the needs of the case, the amount in controversy, limitations on the parties' resources, and the importance of the issues at stake in the litigation."

If the opposition demands another deposition of you, ask the court to rule on whether you must comply.

CONCLUSIONS

Consider the deposition as a trap. It can drag on for unreasonable periods of time. It's important to think and speak effectively in your deposition even though you're tired, frustrated, and want to end the deposition quickly.

More hints for keeping facts straight during your deposition are given in the next chapter.

REFERENCES

1. Flamm MB: What law schools teach about doctors. *Medical Economics* 1983, Feb 21.
2. Johnson LG: The 10 deadly deposition sins, *American Bar Association Journal* 1984;70(Sept):62-66.

8

TRICKY QUESTIONS TO COUNTER DURING THE DEPOSITION

Many factors can cause you to give innacurate answers in a deposition or distort the accurate testimony you do give. If you make seemingly inaccurate, incomplete, or inconsistent statements, it will be noted in the transcript. You may be asked to explain why you made your untrue statements later at the bargaining table or in front of a jury.

The problem is that physicians aren't familiar with legal questioning techniques. The distinction between unavoidable and deliberately caused confusion becomes blurred when unavoidable sources of confusion are deliberately made worse by the opposition.

Here are the sometimes unavoidable—but often deliberate— ways the truth of your deposition statements can be undermined.

WHEN THE OPPOSITION USES POORLY DEFINED TERMS

Don't allow the opposition to cause you to agree to questions such as, "Before the operation the patient was healthy, wasn't he?" Say that "healthy" is a vague term and hard to define.

Don't allow the opposition to trick you into making statements that make you seem biased against the patient, as when you apply poorly defined labels to a person. These labels can be taken out of context and brought up at the bargaining table or the trial to imply that you didn't like or care about the patient.

Example: Let's say that a patient of yours didn't do well, largely because of failure to take medication and keep appointments. Don't directly answer the question, "Mr. Jones was unreliable, wasn't he?" Most leading questions, like this one, are traps. To agree with the statement would give the opposition a damaging statement that could easily be used to imply you didn't like Mr. Jones. To say that Jones was reliable would be untrue and would make it difficult to claim that he contributed to his own problems.

The question is best answered by insisting that the questioning be more specific. Your answer would be: "I would not want to label anyone as being unreliable based on a small number of observations. If you have specific questions concerning how reliably he took medications or kept appointments, I could tell you what actually happened."

Avoid making statements that are open to interpretation because you said, "I guess," "I suppose," "It is possible that," or "As near as I could tell." Such terms suggest you're not sure of what you're saying.

Tip: Consider the medical, legal, and common meanings of all words used. Avoid being tricked into making (or agreeing to) statements that might anger a jury if taken out of context.

Remember that the questions asked of you along with your answers can be read to the jury if your case goes to trial. The plaintiff's attorney is looking for quotes that can damage your image and case. The following series of deposition questions and answers illustrates how to handle questions with negative implications that could be later quoted to a jury to damage your case. Many of these questions have negative implications because of the multiple or emotional meanings of certain words used in the questions.

Q. Why did your knife sever the ulnar nerve?
A. I had no knife.

(You were using a scalpel. Don't let the dialogue support the image of a butcher. Also, was the nerve cut, or did post operative swelling damage it?)

Q. You feel sorry, don't you, for a woman in her 30s who will need to wear a colostomy bag for the rest of her life?
A. I don't understand the question.

(The word "sorry" can suggest guilt, as in "I'm sorry I stepped on your toe.")

Q. What do you think of alcoholics?
A. I don't understand your question.

(You sent home an alcoholic who had been to the emergency department every day for the last two weeks with chest pain. On the night he died you didn't get an electrocardiogram. You should be willing to answer reasonably specific questions about an alcoholic's memory, ability to feel pain, ability to communicate, or whatever. However, as a physician you don't have any opinions about alcoholics in general. If you do, they will be quoted to the jury, describing your motive for causing the poor man to die.)

Q. (Before the deposition starts): Isn't it terrible the way young people are using illegal drugs today?

A. Say nothing before the deposition starts. After it has started, reply if asked this question, "I don't understand the question."

(Even if your injured patient wasn't using drugs, but especially if she was, any answer to the affirmative could indicate a callous attitude on your part.)

Q. You don't remember exactly what you told Mr. Smith when you obtained his consent, do you?

A. I remember what we talked about.

(No one remembers anything "exactly").

Q. What did your attorney instruct you to say about this issue?

A. He told me to tell the truth.

Q. Ever since Mr. Smith had surgery he's had terrible scars.

A. (Silence. . .no question was asked).

WHEN THE OPPOSITION ASKS FOR TOTAL RECALL

The plaintiff's attorney may want to find out all there is to know about the case, yet realize that he's not sure just what questions to ask. Also, there may be documents he's unaware of that should be "discovered." So you may be asked: (1) if your testimony so far reflects your complete knowledge of the subjects covered; (2) if there are any documents that would help you remember more; (3) if anything else was done; or simply (4) "Is that all?"

When asked such questions, think back and see whether your answers have been incomplete or inaccurate. If necessary, ask the reporter to read aloud certain questions and answers. If you want to correct or add to a statement, do so.

Once you're satisfied that your answers are complete and accurate and all relevant issues have been discussed, don't fall into the trap of saying "That is all." If you do later remember additional information or if further reflection changes your opinion about an issue, you could be held accountable for your statement "That is all." It's preferable to say, "That is all I can remember at this time." Or, "Right now I can't remember anything else."

You might say, "We've covered many subjects and jumped from topic to topic, so it's hard to say if we missed anything." This sounds picky, but recording your conversation word for word, making you sign it and swear that it's true, and bringing it to court is also picky.

In some jurisdictions, asking if there's anything else a witness would like to add or if there are any topics that haven't been discussed is considered improper. If this is true in your area, your attorney can object to such questions.[1]

WHEN THE OPPOSITION ASKS FOR JUST A YES OR NO ANSWER

There's nothing wrong with saying you'll try to comply with this request, but don't commit yourself to it. If answering just Yes or No to a question makes your answer incorrect or incomplete, your testimony won't be truthful. Though it's sometimes done in the movies, no one can force you to answer with just a Yes or a No.

You may be interrupted after saying Yes or No in response to a question. You want to qualify or otherwise finish your answer, but the plaintiff's attorney interrupts you and starts talking. Let him say what he wants or ask his next question. Don't interrupt him or enter into a shouting match to get the floor. Wait until he's finished, and then say that you must finish answering the previous question because your answer is incomplete due to the interruption.

WHEN YOU FEEL THE NEED TO SPEAK TOO SOON

Some attorneys recommend a pause of five seconds before answering each question. There are several reasons to hesitate before answering. The pause gives your attorney time to object to the question and time for you to think. You must consider all the ramifications of the question and of your answer before speaking. Chapter 13 tells you how to become practiced in doing this quickly.

Delaying too long in answering every question may be interpreted as a deliberate attempt to interfere with the deposition. The reporter may record the length of pauses. Sometimes pauses of ten seconds or more will labeled as being "long." The transcript can then be taken to a judge to support the claim that you're not cooperating with the proceedings.

On the other hand, you can delay in answering much more during the deposition than you would want to in front of a jury. You don't want to be too slow in answering in front of the jury because they might get the impression that you're not sure of yourself or that you're trying to hide something. Such considerations aren't important in the deposition because you're not trying to impress anyone. You're just trying to make the deposition record be a document that can't be used against you.

Reminder: In the deposition, you can make requests for clarification much more often than a jury would tolerate. Such requests would include insisting that terms be defined, questions not be too general, statements be reworded until clear, etc.

WHEN YOU'RE ASKED MULTIPLE QUESTIONS

Take one at a time. For example, you may be asked, "Did you see the patient on Saturday, take X-rays, and then send her home?" Unless the answers are all in the affirmative, you may need to request that the questions be repeated, one at a time. If you do answer all the questions together, do so in complete sentences to avoid confusion.

WHEN YOU'RE ASKED LEADING QUESTIONS

A leading question instructs you how to answer or puts words into your mouth. Leading questions can cause you to phrase information in the form of an admission. You should especially suspect you're being led into making an admission when the opposing attorney re-phrases information you've given and asks if his statement is correct.

Leading questions often begin with a phrase like "Wouldn't you say that. . . ." Also suspect that a question is leading when the statement ends with a phrase such as "Isn't that true?" or "Wouldn't that have been the proper course of action?" *Don't be eager to agree to a seemingly reasonable question.*

Don't agree to generalizations. Your agreement will be taken out of context. Point out how your case was different or how every medical case is different, making generalizations inaccurate.

Example: One physician was questioned in a deposition about an elective surgical procedure he'd performed on a woman's face in his office. The surgical wound had become infected, giving a very poor result. He was asked if the chance of infection would have been less if the procedure had been performed in the hospital. He said that it probably was.

When pushed to explain why he'd performed such surgery under less optimal conditions, the physician said that the patient had wanted to save money. The deposition thus contained statements by the defendant physician implying that the chance of infection would have been less had the procedure been done in the hospital.

That physician hurt his case. He should have said that the infection rate is reasonably low for such office procedures, and the standard practice is that such procedures are often done in offices. He might have said that his multiple scrub procedures in the office made his infection rate lower than that obtained by some physicians in the hospital.

Actually, the physician did make these face-saving statements later in the deposition. But he'd also been led into making the damaging statements.

Reminder: The plaintiff's attorney will bring up only your damaging statements at the bargaining table and in court. So don't be led into making damaging statements even if you feel you can later explain them away. In this example, the physician should have answered that leading question by saying that because of his meticulous surgical scrubs the infection rate in his office was thought to be as good as that obtained by most physicians in the hospital.

In the following example from a deposition, a defendant's expert witness expertly refuses to let words be put in his mouth. Taking a hint from the defendant's attorney, he "refuses" to answer a question by claiming he doesn't understand it:

Patient's attorney: What opinion did the defendant, Dr. Smith, ask you to give here today?

Defendant's attorney: I object to the form of the question.

Expert witness: I don't understand your question.

Moral: Be careful when answering leading questions.

WHEN YOU'RE ASKED ARGUMENTATIVE QUESTIONS

When questioning disputes your previous answers more than once or twice, the questioning is argumentative. If your attorney doesn't stop argumentative questioning, don't let it upset you. Just be careful not to give out new information in response to the same old questions.

WHEN YOU'RE ASKED QUESTIONS ASSUMING FACTS NOT IN EVIDENCE

Some questions make statements that your attorney should object to. For example, the plaintiff's attorney may say, "What did you do when you saw the patient get worse after three days of your treatment?" The question can't be answered if the patient didn't follow your treatment during those three days. Your answering the question may be taken as an agreement that the patient did follow your instructions. Questions that assume untrue facts should be objected to.

In one case (Love v. Wolf, 1964, 226 CA2d 378, 390, 38 CR 183, 189) a physician was being questioned about the harmful effects of an antibiotic that had injured a patient. The questioning attorney appeared to be reading from a document held in his hand: "In the survey of Dr. (Y), do you recall that 21 of the 29 patients were already dead before his survey was completed? Do you remember that?" In fact, 21 of the patients did not die, and the lawyer wasn't reading from the paper as he appeared to be. Fortunately, an examination of the document being "read" was requested. This underhanded method of stating facts not in evidence was exposed.[2]

Tip: When an attorney refers to a chart, book, or any other piece of evidence, you should examine it yourself. If the opposition appears upset that you take time to examine the evidence, suspect that there is all the more reason to examine it.

WHEN YOU'RE ASKED QUESTIONS THAT DEFINE PROPER CARE

One of the major issues in your case is whether or not you gave proper care. Sit back and think every time you're asked, "Is it not proper to do such-and-such when a patient has this condition?" If your case was similar to that described but critical issues of your case aren't mentioned, say, "That depends on several factors." Or say that you don't understand the question because the case isn't fully described. Your attorney may be able to object to such misleading questions.

There are alternative treatments in medicine. Many conditions can be treated by a variety of different drugs, therapies, and surgical techniques.

Example: One family practitioner delivered a breech baby vaginally. The child had severe neurological deficits. Professors of obstetrics from a nearby medical school testified that the baby should have been monitored electronically and then delivered by Caesarean because of distress. The family practitioner convinced the jury that the ten hours he'd spent in the hospital monitoring the child's progress were as good as electronic monitoring (Boronson, 1985).

The doctor would have damaged his case if during deposition he'd said that the accepted standard of practice is to electronically monitor breech babies.

WHEN YOU'RE ASKED QUESTIONS ABOUT AUTHORITATIVE REFERENCES

Don't give any information to the opposition about what you usually read, what you claim to know, or what books you refer to and believe in. If you claim that you believe or know what is in a certain journal or book, the opposition will find something in the publication you don't know or that disagrees with what you did. This can be embarrassing, especially in front of a jury.

You'll probably be asked what publications you read to learn of developments in medicine. This may seem irrelevant to determining the facts of the case being investigated, but somehow attorneys have gotten the right to force physicians to answer long lists of such questions. Answer them in a way that won't hold you to memorizing and agreeing with the contents of any publications simply because you've claimed you read them.

It's safest to tell the truth: You read from dozens of different journals as your interests lead you. Some publications you get in the mail, many not at your request, so you can't even name them. Dozens of other journals you occasionally read are in the hospital library. A good part of your learning and keeping up to date comes from discussions with other physicians, though you would be hard pressed to remember the number, dates, or specific contents of such discussions.

Caution: Be especially wary when asked if a publication is "authoritative." This means that it's accurate in every sense of the word and up to date. You'll be shown to be incorrect if you claim that any book or journal is accurate. Every journal contains varied opinions, case studies that illustrate what doesn't usually occur and research reports that can't be duplicated. Books are often out of date before they're printed. Be honest in saying that you're willing to comment on the accuracy of any statement from any publication, but each fact has to be considered one at a time.

In your deposition or in court you may be read a statement without being told its source. If you don't agree with the statement and it's from a source you've said was authoritative, your testimony will obviously be inconsistent.

You may say that an author or book is respected, held in high esteem, or an excellent source of information. Again, never agree that anyone or any work is authoritative. The legal definition of that word just doesn't apply in the inexact sciences (such as medicine).

Expert witnesses can also be cross-examined on references they've referred to, considered, or relied on in forming an opinion. An expert is entering a trap when he states that he referred to a textbook in forming an opinion. The opposition may well read a passage from the text that disagrees with the beliefs of the expert and get him to admit this. The opposition will then state that the expert has based his conclusions on a text that reaches contrary conclusions.[3]

An expert, like you, wouldn't be held to such ridiculous implications if he were to claim that his opinions were based on his experience, various medical literature, and conversations with other physicians.

Special case: An expert witness disagreed with a book he had co-authored not long ago. When questioned about this, he claimed that he'd disagreed with the other author about the issue when the book was being written, and he still disagreed.

In the following quote from a malpractice deposition, the plaintiff's attorney tries to get the physician to name a reference on which the physician bases his clinical decisions. He could then find something in it the physician disagreed with.

Attorney: Doctor, where did you learn that feeling the trachea was a reliable means of finding a tension pneumothorax?

Physician: It's just a test to see the result of the tension.

Attorney: Where did you learn this test? What is the origin of the test?

Physician: I've been doing the test for as long as I can remember.

Attorney: Do you know of any text that would describe this test?

Physician: I don't know of any textbooks that mention it.

Attorney: Where is the test recommended?

Physician: I don't know.

Attorney: Do you know anyone else who uses this test?

Physician: I have told other physicians about the results of this test when I describe patients to them. Other physicians over the years have told me they think it is a good test.

The attorney persisted in digging for an authoritative reference, and the physician was persistent in not giving one.

The plaintiff's attorney may say: "There are libraries full of books on medical subjects. Are you telling me not one is authoritative?" You should answer: "Certain texts are authoritative on certain subjects. I couldn't say if any text was authoritative on a subject without being directed to a specific point."

WHEN YOU AND EXPERT WITNESSES ARE ASKED HYPOTHETICAL QUESTIONS

A traditional method of eliciting the opinion of an expert is by use of the hypothetical question. Though it's often asked of experts, you (the defendant) may be asked a hypothetical question to demonstrate your medical knowledge or lack of it. Your answers may be used to show that you didn't treat the plaintiff in the proper manner. You may be present during the depositions of expert witnesses who testify about the care you gave and advise your attorney during such depositions.

The hypothetical question allows the expert witness to comment on a case without giving a final judgement on the case itself. This indirect way of commenting on a case leaves room for the judge and jury (and attorneys at the bargaining table) to interpret the case for themselves.

A hypothetical question needn't contain all the evidence in a case, but it must contain essential facts and issues. If the hypothetical question differs from the actual case in a significant way, an objection should be made. The question may then be restated. If no objection is made, there may be difficulty in later claiming that the hypothetical question was inaccurate.[4]

Hypothetical questions may be objectionable because they omit important facts of the case, assume facts not in evidence (not proven and agreed upon), or are otherwise inaccurate. Your attorney's objection should contain a hint for you. He might say he objects to the hypothetical question because it assumes facts not in evidence. You would then say you can't answer the question until the facts of the case are corrected. If forced to answer the question as it is, you would preface your answer with a statement as to why the question differs from the plaintiff's case. Courts may limit or not accept expert testimony based on a hypothetical question.

Example: One court held that a psychiatrist can give an opinion only after a clinical examination, and a hypothetical question requiring a personal interview wasn't desirable (People v. McIntyre (1967) 256 CA2d 894, 900, 64 Cal Rptr 530). In a contrasting opinion in another case, an expert psychiatrist was allowed to base an opinion on reports and opinions of other physicians (People v. Schindler (1969) 273 CA2d 624 623, 78 Cal Rptr 633).

It's routine for the trial attorney to ask the witness to assume the truth of the facts given in the hypothetical question. In court, it's up to the jury to evaluate the validity of the facts in the question. Many experts won't "just assume" any hypothetical facts they're given, and you shouldn't either.[5]

A hypothetical question can be so complex that an expert witness has to be given the question to study before his deposition. If the hypothetical question (a model of your case) was studied by the opposition's expert in preparation for his deposition, have your attorney ask the expert how long he spent considering the problem. How much time was put into consulting references, asking others, or debating the issues? Bring this up later at the bargaining table or in court to show how difficult it was for the expert to decide what the proper course of action was in your case, even in retrospect.

If the expert answers a complex hypothetical question within seconds of hearing it for the first time, your attorney may be able to show he made a snap judgement based on incomplete understanding of the case. To do this it might only be necessary to ask him to repeat facts of the case. If he can't remember them, his judgement may be based on considerations other than facts of the case.

Whether or not the expert has had a long time to study the hypothetical question, he can be asked about it. Make sure that during the opposing witness's deposition your attorney questions him about which facts of the hypothetical question were relevant to his decision. Without him being able to read over the question, just using his knowledge and understanding, what are the important facts of the case? If it can be shown that the expert didn't understand or take into account important information, his testimony will be weakened. To explore the issue further, you attorney may say: "You omitted facts A, B, and C. Do you consider them important as far as your opinion is concerned?"[6]

Avoiding hypothetical questions: Steer clear of them when possible. Take a long time to think about one if you have to answer it. At times, the facts won't seem reasonable or similar to the facts of your case. If so, say that the case is different than yours or that you don't believe you can comment on an impossible situation. Or say that you must know more details before you can form an opinion. The plaintiff's attorney will have to ask what details you need; you can then bring up the missing items.

If pressed to answer a hypothetical question, you may say you never treat hypothetical patients, and you're not used to prescribing treatment without speaking to and examining a patient.

Another way to avoid answering a hypothetical question is to state that you have no opinion about the question. In effect, you'll be claiming that you don't know what you would do in he described situation. This may make you look dumb or confused, but the position may well be justified if the hypothetical question is long, complex, or different from your own case.

WHEN YOU'RE ASKED QUESTIONS CALLING FOR A NARRATIVE ANSWER

Your attorney should object to questions that require you to tell a long story. Questions should be more specific. If your attorney's objection is overruled, say you don't know exactly what the opposition wants you to comment about.

WHEN YOU'RE ASKED QUESTIONS THAT MISQUOTE YOU

Listen carefully when the opposition quotes anyone, especially you. Ask the reporter to read the statements to you, if necessary. Ascertain their accuracy first, and then worry about answering any questions.

If a question inaccurately repeats a previous statement of yours, you must correct the mistake if your attorney doesn't. Don't hesitate to seek proof of the prior statement if it doesn't sound right. The opposition may become enraged at your request, but remember that it's the "opposition" you're dealing with.

Caution: Improper quoting of previous statements is a common and serious problem in malpractice depositions! So listen carefully when the plaintiff's attorney summarizes what you've said and bases a further question on that. He may be rephrasing your words in the form of an admission. You're not required to go along with simplifications or other restatements of fact. For example:

Q. Doctor, you said that after the patient developed a fever, you ordered the penicillin and the patient's blood pressure dropped. Is penicillin effective treatment for a strep infection?

A. Your question seems to imply that my ordering penicillin caused the patient's blood pressure to drop.

Q. I'm not implying that. Now please answer the question.

A. What is the question you want me to answer?

Q. Is penicillin an effective treatment for a strep infection?

A. If given in adequate doses for a long enough time, yes.

Moral: Don't go along with statements that imply causation or statements that incorrectly quote you.

WHEN YOU'RE ASKED QUESTIONS THAT BEAR ON HEARSAY EVIDENCE

There will be many issues you know about simply because they've been written in the patient's medical record. Don't testify as to accuracy of nurse's notes, information others told you, and statements the patient made that were described in the chart by others. Answer questions about such items by saying you have no first-hand knowledge of them. If asked what the medical record says about a topic, preface your statement with "According to the note in the chart made by Nurse Smith. . .." If this isn't done, you'll be held accountable for the inaccuracies of others.

On the other hand, it's proper to testify that you believed and made decisions based on the observations of others, if that's what happened. It's acceptable medical practice to make treatment decisions based on the observations of other doctors and nurses. If some of those observations were inaccurate, it may explain why your treatment didn't work out.

WHEN YOU'RE ASKED AMBIGUOUS QUESTIONS

Say you don't understand when asked a question that could lead to misinterpretation of your answer. An example of an ambiguous question is, "You don't know if you knew you left the sponge in, do you?" Any answer is open to several interpretations.

Even a question with one negative in it can lead to confusion. "You never did a neurosurgery rotation, isn't that right?" The answer Yes might mean that the statement is right, or that you did take the rotation. When you hear a negative in a question, look for an area of potential confusion.

WHEN YOU NEED TO CLARIFY THE QUESTION AS PART OF THE ANSWER

If a question is long or complex, you may ask that it be reworded. Another way to clarify a question is to restate it in your own words in your reply. For example, "What inquiries and investigations did you make into the complaints and well-being of the patient?" might be clarified and answered by, "My workup of the patient's abdominal pain included a history, physical examination, and laboratory tests." This answer doesn't admit to the fact that you were interested in the general "well-being" of the patient; the only complaint you knew of was the abdominal pain.

Repeating the question when you answer can give you time to think. For example, "When did you first see the patient?" Instead of saying, "Four p.m. on Saturday," you might say, "I first saw the patient at 4 p.m. on Saturday." This tactic, if not used too frequently, may be less objectionable than pausing for long periods before you answer. The amount of question repeating that can be done is limited, but not to the extent it would be when testifying in front of a jury.

Tip: Unless questions are short and simple, your meaning will be clearer if you speak in complete sentences.

WHEN YOU ANSWER QUESTIONS SPECULATIVELY

If you don't know the answer to a question, say so. An example of a question that asks you to speculate is, "Did the patient refuse treatment because he was drunk?" It's proper to have made treatment decisions based on the opinion that the patient was drunk, but it's not proper to speculate about the confused thought processes of the patient in order to answer this question.

In the following quote from a malpractice deposition, the physician speculates a number of times about facts he isn't sure of.

Attorney: Doctor, were you told that the patient you were to examine was being treated for diabetes?

Physician: I believe so.

Attorney: Did you write anything down when you spoke to the referring physician?

Physician: No.

Attorney: Do you remember where you were when speaking to the referring physician?

Physician: Probably in the hospital.

Attorney: And after you saw the patient, where were you when you again met the referring physician?

Physician: I don't remember unless maybe it was in the hospital again.

There is no reason to give such possibly inaccurate testimony.

Just say you don't remember. Statements proven to be inaccurate can be brought up later to embarrass you.

During a recent malpractice deposition, a physician was asked who wrote the hospital policy and procedure manuals for the hospital and emergency department in which he worked. He said he thought a committee wrote the hospital manuals and that the head nurse in the emergency department wrote those manuals. However, after the deposition, he said that he wasn't at all sure who wrote any of the manuals. His guessing did no one any good.

The same physician was asked how much time he spent with the patient who was suing him. He said he couldn't say because he was dividing his time between several patients at once, running from room to room in the E.R. The attorney showed indignant disbelief in the doctor's inability to give a time estimate. The attorney asked if the physician was sure he'd spent more than five minutes but less than an hour with the patient. The physician said Yes. The attorney asked if he'd spent more than ten minutes but less than an hour with the patient. Not wanting to say he'd spent a total of less than ten minutes with the patient, the physician answered Yes, he'd spent over ten minutes with the patient.

The physician didn't remember the encounter three years before. However, he realized that if he said he wasn't sure he'd spent ten minutes with the patient, the statement would look bad in front of a jury.

Moral: You may be pushed into a corner by difficult questions, but avoid speculation. Just say you don't recall.

WHEN YOU NEED TO REFRESH YOUR MEMORY

You'll need to do that by looking at the medical record in order to answer some questions. This can be done as often as needed, though it slows the proceedings. If you must look at the chart frequently or for long periods of time, it implies that you don't remember major facts about the case or the medical theory involved. This will be documented in the deposition transcript.

Caution: If you must refer to the chart to verify a large number of items, the transcript can be used to prove you are deliberately delaying the proceedings.

Studies have shown that most people don't accurately remember what they saw even a short while ago. So it's virtually impossible to remember details of what happened long ago. As a result, a whole set of legal rules and practices have developed concerning the proper way to refresh one's memory.

Legally, when you refresh your memory, you must refer to something that reminds you of what you originally knew: a transcript of a deposition you gave years ago, a note you wrote, or an X-ray you previously looked at. Nevertheless, there will be times when nothing will succeed in refreshing your memory. If the plaintiff's attorney is angry or unbelieving, don't be intimidated into saying you remember something when you don't. The law recognizes such memory lapses.

Caution: If you fail to remember much beyond what is written in the medical records, the plaintiff's attorney may ask you if you're basing all your testimony on the written record. He'll ask if you have any independent recollection of the case. It's a mistake to say that your testimony is based totally on the medical record.

You can say several things in reply to the accusation that you have no basis for your testimony besides the written record:

1. You can say that you know your usual practices and can testify that they're relevant to the case. For example, you know that in addition to writing an NPO note in the chart, you always tell preoperative patients to have nothing to eat or drink after midnight. You're sure you reminded the patient in this case to remain NPO, though you don't remember doing it.
2. You can assert that you may remember more facts about the case after it is discussed further. Your memory might be refreshed by further discussion.

Reminder: The deposition isn't a memory contest. You do have the right to review the record to refresh your memory. Don't be intimidated by the opposition claiming that you don't remember anything because you have to look at the chart. But remember, he'll nail you if you make any wrong statements. That's probably why he's rushing you.

WHEN YOU'RE ASKED QUESTIONS THAT MAKE FALSE STATEMENTS

Don't automatically agree with statements made by the attorney questioning you. In the following example, the attorney is reading from the patient's chart. The physician corrects the attorney's improper interpretations of what he's reading.

Attorney: What is Talwin?
Physician: A medicine given for pain.

Attorney: The chart says that the patient had Talwin at 3 a.m. He was having pain then, right?

Physician: A little pain.

Attorney: At 4 a.m. he was having more pain, isn't that so?

Physician: No. The chart says the patient slept without further medication.

Attorney: I see.

Moral: The physician avoided making the admission that the patient's pain wasn't controlled with Talwin. It would have been a false admission.

WHEN QUESTIONING SEEKS TO PLACE THE BLAME

"If something has gone wrong, it must be someone's fault," the saying goes. If a person is given an anesthetic and suffers a burn to the back, someone must take the blame. The anesthesiologist will say that the scrub nurse must not have put enough electrode jelly on the electrode on the back. The scrub nurse will say the anesthesiologist turned the machine on too high. The ansethesiologist will say the physician used the cautery improperly. *The plaintiff's attorney will sit back, take notes, and collect from everyone.*

If no clear cause for an event can be proven, don't make up stories or assign fault. The astute clinician sees medical happenings nearly every week that he can't explain. Medicine being an inexact science, many of the facts in any given case are usually not known or understood.

Example: In one recent case, a woman with a chronic back problem was undergoing an epidural block for pain control. She emerged with footdrop and sued the anesthesiologist for $400,000. The defense was that no one really knew why the footdrop resulted. The needle might have hit a nerve root, and this can happen no matter how careful the physician is. Honesty, offering an explanation for what might have happened, and lack of finger-pointing won the case for the physician.

Two common tricks are used to encourage you to point the finger of blame. (1) The plaintiff's attorney will speak in such a way as to indicate that he already realizes the fault lies with a certain other person. He's merely obtaining details about the event from you. (2) The plaintiff's attorney speaks in such a way as to assume that the unfortunate event was your doing, but he could see why it happened.

No blame could be associated with the event; it just happened that way.

Caution: Beware of those easy questions that subtly point the finger of blame.

WHEN QUESTIONS TRY TO MAKE YOU A MIND READER

When you hear a question that asks you to read someone's mind, realize that the question is a trap. For example, "Why did the patient refuse treatment?" The person might have told you she had to stay home to take care of her children. In many cases, however, the person is really afraid of hospitals, concerned about the cost, not willing to interrupt a drug or drinking habit, or unwilling to have painful tests done.

When asked about other people's motivations, reasons, or thoughts, watch out. The opposition may be trying to make you limit the issues in the case. Tell the attorney that you can't read minds. If asked what the patient told you her reason was for refusing treatment, you can tell that. But leave the possibility open for the existence of other reasons causing the patient's actions and the failure of your treament.

WHEN YOU'RE ASKED QUESTIONS THAT MAKE YOU A JUDGE

A physician was asked in a recent deposition, "What was the demeanor of the patient?" Such legal language is confusing. Beyond that, however, realize that a trap is being set when you're asked to judge a plaintiff or a relative of a plaintiff.

If you make degrading remarks, they can be taken out of context when your unfortunate patient is dressed up in court, looking respectable in front of the jury. You might have described the patient as "a dirty, obnoxious drunk who had not taken a bath in a month." You might be right, but you'll lose your case when your deposition statement is read in court. Especially if the patient's attorney has explained how his head-injured client hadn't had that much to drink and had been beaten by robbers in a dirty alley.

When asked to describe a patient, be objective. Make no judgements (that you tell anyone about). "He was covered with mud. His underwear had old urine stains on them. He wouldn't cooperate with treatment. He tried to punch the nurse in the jaw. His blood alcohol level was three times the legally intoxicated level."

Moral: These types of statements aren't judgemental on your part. They put the patient in proper focus.

WHEN QUESTIONS CONTAIN WORDS WITH SEVERAL MEANINGS

There are several different meanings of such words as possible, probable, following, and prove. These terms have legal, medical, and common meanings. You can be held to the legal and medical interpretations of what you say. Your statements can be read to the jury, but only the common meanings of the words would be understood by the jurors. Here are four examples:

1. In legal and medical terms, "possible" means that a thing can happen. In common terms, the word might mean anything, depending on how it's used: "It's very possible the patient would have lived had the treatment been different."
2. In civil law, something is "probable" or "likely" if its chances of happening are more than 50 percent. Again, the lay person's interpretation of these terms is unclear.
3. The word "following" can imply causation: "The patient had a cardiac arrest following initiation of anesthesia." Any wording that describes one event preceeding another can imply causation.
4. "Proofs" are different in science, mathematics, and law. In science, all relevant facts are considered and logically used to show the truth of an assertion. In law, each side considers the facts, case precedents, and laws supporting that side's interests. In mathematics, proof is a logically airtight argument showing that an assertion must be true. In common terms, proof is whatever convinces a listener.

Thus the truth in law isn't an absolute one as in mathematics or pure science. An attorney, if he's a good advocate, is totally biased and committed to his client's cause. If he were a seeker of truth, he would have been a scientist, not an attorney. The attorney is a manipulator of the spoken word; he's an applied psychologist. *He wants money and victory.* He wants to please his client and impress his peers.

Reminder: Many plaintiff's attorneys see themselves as agents of the poor, the oppressed, the neglected. They believe they've improved the standards of medical care through malpractice suits.

They're not concerned with cost-effective medical care or the contributory negligence of their clients. They're cynical.

To meet them on their own terms, keep in mind that your words during deposition will be viewed from a perspective much different than your own. You must be unambiguous, consistent, and accurate. Avoid estimating anything. You may be asked to "estimate" how many patients you've treated with conditions similar to that in the case being discussed. You may be asked to "estimate" what percentage of patients respond to the treatment you gave. If you give a different answer, the attorney can read your contrary answer from the deposition transcript. You "estimate" can be shown to be inconsistent and potentially inaccurate. You testimony in general will then be in question.

Moral: Don't estimate, guess, or otherwise try to be nice to the opposition by supplying answers about things you're not sure of. If you don't know something, say you don't know it. If pushed to answer a question that's open to several interpretations, ask that the question be restated or say that you're not sure what the question means.

WHEN QUESTIONS CONTAIN UNKOWN TERMS

At times, you won't know the meaning of a word. Trial lawyer Ellis Kahn of Charleston, S.C., laughs every time he thinks of the easiest malpractice case he ever handled. "I was taking a pretrial deposition from a doctor my client was suing for an appendicitis death. I went through a bunch of routine questions and then asked offhandedly, 'Don't you agree, Doctor, that the cause of your patient's death was iatrogenic?' "

"It sure was!" he agreed. *Disaster!*

In this case, the physician wouldn't admit ignorance of the meaning of "iatrogenic," a term most physicians understand as "medically induced," but not this doctor.

Caution: Make sure you understand the terms you're using. If you don't know the meaning of a word, you may be more embarrassed if you don't admit your ignorance than if you did.

WHEN YOU'RE QUESTIONED ABOUT UNFAMILIAR DOCUMENTS

Unknown documents, as well as unknown words, can get you into trouble. The plaintiff's attorney may hand you a document and start questioning you about it. The document may be your hospital's by-laws, your malpractice insurance policy, the consent form signed by your patient, or a medical article. If you take time to read the document before answering, the attorney may act annoyed and say you're delaying the proceedings.

It's a mistake to be railroaded into testifying about a document that isn't fresh in your mind. You do have the right to review a document you're being questioned about. If the plaintiff's attorney is upset about your reviewing document, he probably wants you to incorrectly answer questions about the document.

Tip: Keep the facts straight by taking time to review any material you're questioned about.

WHEN YOU CONFUSE THE COURT REPORTER

Some attorneys will make it difficult for the court reporter to accurately record what happened and what was said at a deposition. Tactics that confuse the reporter are listed in the accompanying table.[7]

BOX 8-1

Actions That Make Deposition Difficult For The Reporter

1. Talking at the same time as someone else.
2. Mumbling, chewing gum, covering one's face with a hand.
3. Talking too softly or quickly.
4. Using foreign words.
5. Using words such as "Uhh-huh."
6. Shaking the head and using other gestures.
7. Pointing to anatomical models, entries in a medical chart, or other objects and saying "This" or "Here" without defining it.
8. Using words that sound like other words.

Don't let such tactics work against you. If you suspect that one of these tactics has kept the reporter from accurately recording what has occurred or been said, ask that the transcript be read so he confusion can be corrected.

CONCLUSIONS

We've discussed many tricky questions to counter during your deposition. These factors are an unavoidable result of our system of legal justice, though their effect can be increased beyond reason by the lawyer questioning you. Just remember the potential these questions have for distorting the meaning of your testimony.

The next chapter deals with a subject, well known to attorneys, that can make concentration during a deposition difficult: your physical comfort during the deposition.

REFERENCES

1. Davis PA: *Discovery Techniques: A Handbook for Michigan Lawyers.* The Institute for Continuing Legal Education, Ann Arbor, Hutchins Hall, 1977.
2. Friedman LR: *Essentials of Cross-Examination.* California Continuing Education of the Bar, 1968, Regents of the University of California, Library of Congress card No 68-63003.
3. Ibid.
4. Brosnahan JJ: Chapter XXIX, Trial handbook for California lawyers, p 142 in *Preparing and Examining Expert Witnesss.* May/June 1978, Program Materials; California Continuing Education of the Bar, Berkeley, California, 1978.
5. Gots RE: *Hypotheticals and the Expert Medical Witness.* Legal Aspects of Medical Practice vol 10, No 1, Jan 1982.
6. Friedman LR: *Essentials of Cross-Examination.* California Continuing Education of the Bar, The Regents of the University of California, 1968.
7. Johnson LG: *The deadly deposition sins.* American Bar Association Journal 70:62-66, Sept 1984.

9

YOU NEED TO AVOID PHYSICAL
DISCOMFORT DURING DEPOSITION

During your deposition, if any of your answers are wrong, inconsistent, incomplete, or otherwise embarassing to you, it will be down in transcript for all to see. So it's extremely important that you not be distracted by physical discomforts.

Considerations important to your physical comfort include deposition length, time of day, posture, smoking in the room, table arrangements, and your physical conditioning. Discuss these considerations with your attorney to see what can be done about them. Changes are more difficult during the deposition, though much can still be done.

HOW LONG WILL IT LAST?

If the deposition were used by the plaintiff's attorney to simply gather and verify information relevant to the case, it wouldn't take very long. Unfortunately, attorneys use long, complex depositions to try to force physicians to make inaccurate statements that will help support the claim of malpractice.

You must be at your peak performance throughout the deposition, which is likely to take many hours. Be especially careful toward the end, when you'll tend to be fatigued.

What if you realize during deposition that you can't handle difficult questioning for many hours? If your powers of concentration wane, have your attorney ask that the deposition be continued at another time, giving the true reason for your request. If your request is denied, make the most of whatever is bothering you to end the meeting: backache, legs hurting, headache, or the flu. As a physician, you've often seen this done by patients wanting a work release. It's a reasonable—and usually acceptable—thing to do when you can't function well.

Final ploy: If you're very uncomfortable because of the length of the deposition, you can and should insist that it be continued at another time. They're not going to take the deposition without you there.

CHOOSING THE DATE AND TIME OF DAY

They're usually set by agreement between attorneys. Often the deposition notice is served, then a discussion is held as to whether the dates and times are convenient for all involved. Attorneys will be concerned about having enough notice to move for protective orders. The potential trial date is an important consideration.

You'll probably want to schedule the deposition so it doesn't interfere with your practice. It's also a good idea to keep it from stealing time from your family life. The ideal time would be during a weekday when your office is customarily closed (and your family is busy). If that isn't possible, consider scheduling it for a morning or afternoon and cancelling your office appointments.

Tip: If you usually work at night, don't be forced into a deposition during the day. Insist that the questioning take place at a time when you're normally awake.

OVERCOMING POSTURE AND SEATING PROBLEMS

Some of us have back problems, and some of us are overweight. If the long hours of sitting cause pain or stiffness, consider occasional breaks or even standing or pacing the floor while being questioned.

A benefit of standing and moving about is that your circulation and powers of concentration will be improved. We often fall asleep in lectures and while watching TV or reading. Few of us ever fall asleep while taking a walk.

Walking the floor wouldn't be advisable in court because members of the jury would wonder about your unusual behavior. The deposition, however, is a different situation. You're not trying to impress or gain favor with the plaintiff's attorney. So walk.

WHAT DO YOU DO ABOUT SMOKING?

If you're addicted to the weed, you won't function well without it. You have the right to be able to smoke, though others may insist on your doing it outside the conference room. During such smoking breaks, you'll have the time to think about the questioning and discuss it with your attorney.

If you don't smoke, it's likely you find it irritating to sit in a room filled with smoke. No one has the right to subject you to such conditions, especially when you're expected to function optimally in answering questions. Have your attorney insist that people abstain or take breaks outside of the room to smoke. Use the break times to relax, move around, and discuss the deposition with your attorney.

Tip: If some people insist on forcing you to breathe smoke during your deposition, let your physical symptoms show: Cough, choke, and take time to wash out your eyes. These interruptions will force others to give your body the respect it's demanding.

BEST SPOT FOR THE CONFERENCE ROOM

The room in which you're questioned should be comfortable, quiet, and private. Don't tolerate distracting noise or sunlight shining in your eyes.

Some physicians have depositions in their own offices. If you're giving an expert opinion in someone else's lawsuit, this might be workable. However, if you're the one being sued, the situation is dangerous. You'll need to give undivided attention to the deposition for long periods of time. You can't be distracted by phone calls, patients who find that you're there but not immediately available, and questions from your secretary.

Holding the deposition in the opposing attorney's office has disadvantages. You may not have ready access to copy machines, telephones, bathrooms, reference books, and secretarial help.

Perhaps the most desirable location for your deposition is your own attorney's office. This assumes he can control outside interruptions. Wherever you are, turn off your beeper and make arrangements for your patients to be taken care of.

Visitors at a deposition can also be distracting. Your state laws may define who can be present at a deposition. The plaintiff's attorney may bring others for the purpose of getting advice. He might want other witnesses or the plaintiff to be there to intimidate you or to learn about the deposition process itself. Ask your attorney to object to this audience to the extent permitted by law.

WHAT HAPPENS AT THE CONFERENCE TABLE

The conference table should be large enough for you and your attorney to sit together and arrange papers relevant to your case. You should be able to whisper to and pass notes to and from your attorney without them being read by the opposition, but keep in mind that the opposition has the right to examine any papers you have at the deposition. If you don't want the opposition to know something, don't put it in writing. If you do whisper to your attorney, make sure the sensitive microphone recording the deposition isn't close by.

Do not sit so close to the questioning attorney that you would feel uncomfortable if he were to stare, shout, or lean toward you. One technique, publicized in the legal literature, is to lean toward a witness, "invading the body space." As long as you keep talking, the opposition will usually physically back off. If you stop talking, he'll lean forward, making you feel the need to keep rambling.

Another way you can be made uncomfortable is by staring. If you find the plaintiff's attorney or anyone else staring at you, realize that it's a deliberate insult designed to weaken your ability to concentrate. There are several things you can do about being stared at:

1. Keep your temper. You might say, on the record, "Mr. Smith's assistant has been staring directly at me for half an hour. Please ask him to stop that."
2. You might say the staring has made you so uncomfortable you want to take break.
3. You might say you need a number of questions repeated because the staring is distracting you.
4. Don't try to please the plaintiff's attorney. Tell him with your eyes and your strength that objectionable behavior will make you even more determined to say as little as possible.

When possible, sit next to your attorney with a corner or a bend in the table between you. In this way you can look at notes with him and still see his facial expressions without turning to look for them during questioning. Your expert witness should also sit near your attorney so that he can assist the attorney during the deposition.

By the same token, avoid sitting directly facing the questioning attorney. Otherwise, he'll need only brief glances to refer or write on the notes in front of him.

Moral: Conference-room and conference-table considerations are complex, sometimes conflicting, and often not a matter of choice. But even if you're not able to arrange the room and seating arrangement to your liking, take comfort in realizing that you're not the first physician in a malpractice case to have had these problems.

THE NEED TO MAINTAIN PHYSICAL CONDITIONING

When an extra, time-consuming stress is thrust on us, the natural tendency is to deteriorate physically. Nervousness makes us eat, drink, and smoke more. Time is stolen from exercise and recreational activities. But it's damaging to your malpractice case if you allow yourself to deteriorate. It's important that you maintain the ability to think clearly under long hours of deposition questioning.

Consider the lawsuit and all the accompanying pressures, indignities, and schedule interruptions to be a challenge. Decide that despite these problems, you'll improve your physical condition. You didn't get to be an M.D. by being weak and capitulative.

Action: Devote at least half an hour every other day to physical conditioning. Start gradually to avoid injury. Get the advice of physicians familiar with exercise and with any physical problems you might have. Hospital physical therapy departments are usually happy to teach exercises to physicians.

Reminder: Lawyers are aware of and make use of the fact that performance deteriorates with fatigue. In one legal text, Georgetown University Law Professor Jeffrey L. Kestler states: "A lengthy, complex proceeding can require almost superhuman effort. If you become fatigued, your sense are dulled, and you have trouble paying attention. If this occurs at a time when your adversary remains keen, then you are at a serious disadvantage. . ... If you are physically fit, you will better be able to stay alert. . ... If you are not fit, you are more likely to break down under strain. . ."[1]

To make the best of your physical condition, don't drink alcohol or take any sedatives before the deposition or during breaks. You may feel that a little Valium would calm your nerves, but if combined with sitting for a long time in a stuffy room, sedatives can nearly put you to sleep.

In sum: Every improvement in your physical conditioning in preparation for the deposition is time well spent—an improvement in your ability to handle the stress and fatigue to be encountered during your deposition.

CONCLUSIONS

Now that you're tuned for peak physical performance, you can go on to the next chapter, which describes psychological manipulations that may be used against you.

REFERENCES

1. Kestler JL: *Questioning Techniques and Tactics.* McGraw-Hill Book Co, New York, 1982, p 14.

10

DEALING WITH THE OPPOSITION'S PSYCHOLOGICAL WARFARE TACTICS

Attorneys are schooled in the tactics of psychological warfare. As we've seen, when used during questioning, these tactics can distract the physician from the important task of answering questions accurately. *Just recognizing a psychological warfare tactic for what it is can blunt its effect.*

"Psychological warfare is an important dimension of litigation. . ... Lawyers must become adept at utilizing psychological tactics offensively in order to gain a competitive edge. In litigation, as in sports, the most commonly encountered methods of psychological subversion are provocation, intimidation, and distraction. Each of these methods is distinctive, requiring different defenses."

That quote from the Trial Practice Series of publications written for attorneys by J.L. Kestler in 1982 tells us that the fear, guilt, and emotional upset felt by so many physicians undergoing deposition questioning is deliberately induced by the opposition. The weapons of psychological warfare may be intended by respected legal practitioners to be used only to obtain the truth from dishonest witnesses. But they're often used for less respectable purposes.

Here's a rundown of the techniques of deposition psychological warfare—and how to fight them.

DEALING WITH PROVOCATION

Provocation is accomplished by behavior that incites, angers, or irritates you. In criminal law, provocation has been defined as words or conduct that lead to a killing in hot passion and without deliberation. On a less dramatic level, provocation is likely to cause you to think about issues other than the next question you must answer. You'll be distracted and not think clearly.

Provocation can be accomplished by insinuations, insults, deliberate misinterpretations of your statements, and the hundreds of other irritations described in this book.

To deal with provocation, you must first recognize it. Then turn your anger into determination and use it as a source of energy, not as a precursor of depression or despair. When you're insulted and your pulse rate increases, think to yourself: "These deliberate insults have a purpose. I must be more careful now and even more suspicious of the motives of the opposition."

DEALING WITH INTIMIDATION

Intimidation is designed to deter from action by inducing fear. Any physician defendant is likely to be intimidated by the manners, poise, and skill of an attorney who has conducted hundreds of depositions.

During the deposition, you may not look or sound very good. You may need to stop to think about things. You may receive impatient looks when you ask that ambiguous questions be rephrased or simplified. Nevertheless, you must do the best you can and ignore any feelings of intimidation.

Moral: When you see a three-piece suit, disciplined legal assistants, and a well-planned attack, realize these were bought with money won from physicians who were intimidated because they lost sight of the real dignity of their own scrub suits and long hours of honest work.

An attorney who described himself as "Attila the Hun in a suit" recently told attorneys how he intimidates physicians into losing malpractice lawsuits. His talk was given at a medical malpractice institute sponsored by the American Bar Association and the American Society of Law and Medicine. "I like to keep the physician off balance. I leap right in like a big lion and start to claw at a major point so that he commits himself too quickly before thinking things through."

This attorney sees the deposition as the single most important part of a malpractice case because the angry or confused physician may make statements that can later be examined by the jury. This attorney holds depositions in his law offices. No coffee is served, and German war memorabilia line the walls.[1]

Reminder: Attorney rhetoric routinely becomes heated in depositions. So make a supreme effort to not take part in angry arguments. When a verbal fight breaks out, sit quietly while the lawyers argue.

In the following excerpt from a malpractice deposition, the defendant doctor's expert witness is being questioned:

Patient's attorney: Have you ever been sued for malpractice?

Expert: I don't know if that question is relevant.

Patient's attorney: It may be. I hope I'm asking relevant questions. I won't waste your time or mine, Doctor. Just answer the question.

Defendant's attorney: I object to any further questions about our expert's past involvement in malpractice cases.

Patient's attorney: I really need to know about this.

Defendant's attorney: I'm not going to sit here and argue about it all day.

Lesson: The physician expert avoided a trap by suggesting that the question warranted an objection. He then sat back and watched the fight.

Another method of intimidation practiced by plaintiff's attorneys is to wait expectantly after a physician has finished answering a question. There is a natural tendency to feel the need to keep talking when the person listening to you seems to expect you to say more. Stop speaking when each question has been answered. Learn to enjoy seeing that your answer hasn't satisfied the opposition's hunger for more information.

Another intimidation tactic is described in a Litigation Course Handbook: "Lawyers employ various tactics in examining witnesses, ranging from charm (in hopes of getting the witness to drop his or her guard) to abuse (in hopes of intimidating the witness). Counsel should prepare the witness for any tactics counsel knows the opposition is likely to use. For example, through design or otherwise, lawyers frequently ask a witness a long list of questions that he or she knows nothing about, either because the questions have nothing to do with the case, or because they concern areas that are not related to the witness's singular role in the case. During deposition preparation, the witness should be counseled not to be embarrassed or disconcerted if he or she must repeatedly answer, 'I don't know.' "[2]

Although it's customary to question defendant doctors about their background, physicians are often intimidated by questions implying that their credentials are inadequate. Consider these questions:

- Doctor, which medical school did you attend?
- Is that medical school accredited?
- Did you graduate?
- Did you fail examinations or courses while in medical school?
- What was your standing in the class?
- Where did you do your internship?
- Was *that* program accredited?
- Where did you do your residency?
- How many patients of this age, taking these medications, who had this complication, did you care for during your training?
- So few?—or—Why did so many patients have that complication where you trained?
- Did you pass your specialty boards the first time?
- In which parts of the specialty board examination did you score the lowest?
- What postgraduate training have you had in areas relevant to (this obscure) aspect of the patient's case?
- How many papers have you authored on this subject?
- Is it true that you have been in medical practice for only X years?
- How many conferences have you attended in the last year on the care of patients such as the one we're discussing?
- Did you have any specialty training in these other areas related to the patient's case?
- Why, then, did you not call in appropriate specialists?

Unless a physician has an exceptional background (and possibly even if he does), such questions will make him feel he's lost the lawsuit before it's begun. Plaintiff's attorneys convey the impression that complete knowledge and competence, and a perfect standard of care, are expected from all physicians at all times. These expectations aren't what the law requires, but that isn't always easy to prove to a jury. No wonder physicians feel intimidated when they're sued!

Tip: When answering questions about your background, remember that your attorney can ask similar questions that will show you in a much better light. If he feels it's important that the deposition transcript show such information, he can question you later to bring out the needed information.

"Depositions serve different functions from those of trial pro-

ceedings, and attorneys will have some liberty to do things differently. Questions may be asked that would be inappropriate or inadmissible at trial, and a hostile attitude, short of harrassment, that would
tactically be bad form at the trial, can be taken toward a deponent.
Questionable attorney conduct can usually be controlled by peer
pressure, by noting such conduct on the record, by asking the offending attorney to stop, and if all else fails, by seeking a protective order
or Rule 37 sanctions. Rule 30(d) describes the situation and procedures available to seek relief from improper conduct by attorney or a
deponent."[3]

Lesson: Recognize intimidation as a nasty trick to throw you off
guard. If you let it anger or scare you, it can lessen your ability to
concentrate and properly answer questions.

DEALING WITH GUILT-CAUSING TACTICS

Perhaps the most frequent comment heard from medical personnel
who have been questioned in depositions is, "That lawyer made me
feel so guilty, even though I know I did nothing wrong." Analysis of
these cases shows that the guilt-provoking questions aren't those
concerned with the facts of the malpractice case in question. Guilt
comes from questions that imply the witness is incompetent or unsure of his testimony.

Example: The physician defendant may be asked repeatedly
about not finishing a residency, being in practice "only" four years,
or not being able to remember supposedly important details of the
case. The plaintiff's attorney may bring up many disturbing and embarassing facts about your education, experience, office address, and
number of procedures performed per year. Unless the matter being
discussed can be proved to be a proximate cause of the damages suffered by the plaintiff, it's worthless to the opposition. So don't be
upset by such questioning.

Don't let guilt color your testimony and cloud your thinking.
When asked embarrassing, insulting questions that have already
been answered, you may choose to just go along with the questioning, comforted by the knowledge that you understand what is happening, and that no new information is being passed on to the opposition.

You may object to such abuse, however, because time is being
wasted on repetitive questions. If the abuse doesn't stop, apply the
methods described elsewhere in this book dealing with repetitive
questions.

Questions that may induce guilt should be carefully answered.

Instead of guilt, they should induce quiet, controlled strength in you. Before your deposition, consider how you would answer the following questions. Ask your attorney if you're not sure of the proper answers.

- When did you last talk to your attorney about this case?
- How many times have you discussed this case with your attorney?
- Have you discussed your testimony or the case with others?
- Have you any financial interest in the outcome of this case?
- Have you taken notes on what you have heard during other depositions?
- Have you studied your (or others') previous depositions?
- Did you meet with any other defendant doctors or nurses to plan a common defense or discuss this case?
- Was a conference with other defendants held in which you were able to refresh each other's memory of what was said and done?

Another guilt-provoking trick is to ask you what your understanding of the oath is. You'll be sworn in at the beginning of the deposition. You may take a question about the oath as an insult (and this may be understandable given the way you're asked about it). Realize that the opposition is simply trying to make you uncomfortable and trying to cause you to make statements that can be used to embarrass you.

Action: Simply answer that the oath means you will tell the truth.

DEALING WITH NONVERBAL TACTICS

You'll be distracted and upset when the attorney questioning you makes faces, shakes his head, or otherwise shows disbelief or disgust at what you say. This effect is heightened when the opposition brings several attorneys, assistants, and witnesses to hear your deposition. If several people are grimacing and shaking their heads during your testimony, you may feel as if you were preaching temperance in a bar on Saturday night.

When this harrassment occurs, wait until two or three persons show their displeasure to a statement at once. Address the transcriber saying, "Please note in the record that after my last answer, Mr. Jones, Smith, and Doe shook their heads and frowned. Please also note in the record that I've endured this harrassment for the last two hours and request that it be stopped." Even if the opposition objects, your statement should be recorded. This may stop the harrassment and will serve as evidence for a later countersuit.

Some witnesses become nervous when the opposition writes notes after certain important questions. The witness feels he's said something wrong. One nurse found that four lawyers would feverishly write on their note pads whenever she answered questions on one critical topic. "I knew they were trying to intimidate me, but I wouldn't change my story. I know what happened, and they weren't going to get me to say anything else, no matter how differently they asked it or how much scribbling they did."

DEALING WITH SPLIT-UP TACTICS

Most plaintiff's attorneys are sensitive enough to realize when you have a disagreement with your own attorney, so they may deliberately spend more time on issues that cause friction between you and your attorney.

Another ploy is to wait until your attorney interrupts you because you're getting into dangerous territory or giving information that needn't be brought up. The opposition will suggest that your attorney doesn't need to interrupt you so rudely because you're an intelligent witness.

Still another technique is to tell you that you needn't follow your attorney's instructions to refuse to answer an improper question. The opposition will say that you're intelligent enough to understand the question, and a lot of time and money will be saved if you would only cooperate.

Naturally, these techniques are meant to cause an emotional distance between you and your attorney. To the extent the techniques are successful, you will ask for less assistance from your attorney. Not only will you be trapped in a deposition, but you will be alone.

Moral: In general, don't disagree with your attorney. If you do, keep it a secret between the two of you. Take a recess and walk around the block if you need to talk to him.

If your attorney objects to a question because it's vague, don't volunteer that you would have no trouble answering it. The question may be dangerous in a way you don't understand. Your attorney is trying to help you limit the amount of harmful information you give the opposition.

DEALING WITH A LOUD OR ABUSIVE TONE OF VOICE

Few attorneys will shout or use a cutting, sarcastic tone of voice when questioning a witness in court. The judge and jury will recognize such behavior and will tend to side with the underdog. But the judge and jury aren't present at a deposition, so these outdated trial techniques of verbal abuse are still sometimes used in depositions.

There are several ways to deal with such abuse. One way is to ignore it. If you're successful, it may cease.

If you can't ignore it, your attorney can object and may succeed in stopping it, at least for a while.

Tip: If the harrassment really doesn't bother you, consider the fact that continuing to insult you will take the opposition's energy and distract him. Don't say anything. Just let him continue for as long as he wants and get carried away with the act. Make sure the court reporter takes note of his tone and loudness of voice, shaking fist, and banging on the table.

DEALING WITH A SHOW OF DISBELIEF

The attorney looks shocked at your answer and says, "Are you sure about that?" You falter and say, "Well, I *think* that's what happened."

How can anyone remember something that happened so long ago? After all, your so-called negligent act took place four years ago.

Some attorneys will act as if you're not telling the truth when they want you to change your story. Don't go along with this tactic. Your reply should be, "Of *course* I'm sure about it."

DEALING WITH TENSION-PRODUCING ACTIVITY

Physicians are famous for yelling at nurses, throwing instruments, and not being under control in times of stress. In the context of having too much work to do, a patient going bad, and the physician being tired, such actions are understandable. When taken out of context, they make the physician look like a fool.

If you feel tension rising, it's time to relax. While a little tension can give you energy to continue a long ordeal, too much tension can distract you. When you feel the ability to concentrate waning, it's time to take a break and relax. Insist on being able to stretch your legs or go to the bathroom.

The opposition may object to breaks in the proceedings, but take them when needed to allow you to think clearly.

Reminder: If the opposition is upset about how long it's taking, they can start questioning in a straightforward manner, stick to the facts of the case, and end the deposition quickly.

Several months before your deposition, take training in relaxation therapy. There are popular books, medical meetings, and cassette tapes available on the subject. Psychiatrists and other counselors you know might teach the method to you or suggest a proper reference.

Relaxation therapy instructional materials contain procedures for relaxing each part of your body, removing unwanted thoughts from your mind, and calming your emotions. After going through the lengthy relaxation sequences a few times, you'll learn how to relax your body and clear your mind in a few seconds.

CONCLUSIONS

Keep your cool! Don't let psychological warfare insults anger you or decrease your powers of concentration.

Your attorney should do most of the objecting when unreasonable pressures are put on you. His objections to unreasonable treatment should be stated openly so that they become part of the deposition transcript. Remember, just knowing that such manipulations are standard practice, and not a result of any supposed deficiency you have, can give you comfort.

Once you've learned how to deal with such treatment, you can concentrate on limiting the amount of information you give the opposition, the subject of our next chapter.

REFERENCES

1. Jancin B: *Family Practice News*, Feb 1-14, 1985.
2. Kennedy RD: Preparing defendant doctor for deposition, in Miller DG: *Taking and Defending Depositions in Personal Injury Cases.* Litigation Course Handbook Series No 236, Practicing Law Institute, 1983, pp 109-123.
3. Haydock RS, Herr DF: *Discovery Practice.* Boston, Little Brown & Co, 1981.

11

DON'T GIVE THE OPPOSITION TOO MUCH INFORMATION

At a recent party someone asked, "Does anyone know what time it is?" Three attorneys nearby said, "Yes." Nobody said what time it was. Though meant as a joke, the incident showed how attorneys are used to thinking. "Just answering the question" is one of the techniques you must apply during your deposition to limit the flow of information to the opposition.

This chapter will discuss techniques used by plaintiff's attorneys to obtain information unfairly. Defensive tactics on your part include the importance of telling the opposition as little as possible, dealing with repetitious questions, avoiding generalities, controlling your body language, the difference between clarification and elaboration, and being comfortable with periods of silence.

HOW TO TELL THE OPPOSITION AS LITTLE AS POSSIBLE

The malpractice deposition is one of the most powerful tools the plaintiff's attorney can use in his effort to sue you. If the information-gathering during a deposition were done in an honest, straightforward way and questioning were restricted to the plaintiff's case, there would be less of a need for the information in this chapter.

But as we've seen, questioning is done in misleading, confusing ways. Sophisticated techniques have evolved over the years that lead physicians to make statements that are easily distorted and taken out of context. In addition, the questioning and observations of the plaintiff's attorney can give information about your past, your attitudes, your practices in other cases, and your personal weaknesses. This information isn't relevant to the process of discovering the facts of the malpractice case in question. In fact, it's none of the opposing attorney's business.

Lesson: The physician should cooperate with questioning that helps establish the facts of the case. But regard any questioning beyond the facts as part of an unreasonable attempt to find damaging material that can be used to embarrass you. It usually won't be apparent just where the questioning is leading or how your statements can be taken out of context and fitted together to damage your case. So it's important that you disclose as little information as possible even though you don't see its danger at the time.

YOUR RIGHT TO REFUSE TO ANSWER QUESTIONS

When answering questions, always pause long enough for your attorney to object to a question. His objections will be based on legal principles. He may want to register his complaint and then let you answer. The objection makes later suppression of the question and its answer possible. Or your attorney may really not want you to answer. If he persists in telling you not to answer a question and the plaintiff's attorney won't modify the question to your attorney's satisfaction, a conflict has arisen that the court having jurisdiction over your malpractice case can settle. The plaintiff's attorney can ask the court to rule on whether or not you should be required to answer.

Questions that have sometimes been judged to be unreasonable are those concerning one's racial background and questions that are argumentative, repetitious, misleading, or irrelevant. Privileged information, such as what you and your attorney have discussed together, needn't and shouldn't be divulged to the opposition.

Reminder: The plaintiff's physician-patient confidentiality, however, needn't be preserved. Your former patient waived the right of privacy when the lawsuit was initiated.

Information that would not be admissible at trial *can* be obtained during deposition. Rule 26(b)(1) of the Federal Rules of Civil Procedure authorizes discovery in "any matter, not privileged, which is relevant to the subject matter involved in the pending action." Information can be discovered if it can reasonably be expected to lead to the discovery of admissible evidence.

What if you don't answer satisfactorily? Rule 37(a) of the Federal Rules of Civil Procedure states:". . .If a deponent fails to answer a question. . .the discovering party may move for an order compelling an answer. . .. An evasive or incomplete answer is to be treated as a failure to answer. . ..If the motion is granted, the court, shall, after opportunity for hearing, require the party or deponent whose conduct necessitated the motion or the party or attorney advising such conduct or both of them to pay to the moving party the reasonable expenses incurred in obtaining the order, including attorney's fees. . ..

"If the motion is denied, the court shall, after opportunity for hearing, require the moving party or the attorney advising the motion or both of them to pay to the party or deponent who opposed the motion for the reasonable expenses incurred in opposing the motion, including attorney's fees . . .."

Courts decide differently, but most will uphold the deponents' refusals to answer questions dealing with privileged information. Courts will also usually back you up if you refuse to answer questions made in bad faith. "Bad faith" questions include those that are embarrassing, harrassing, repetitive, annoying, unclear, misleading, or argumentative (Haydock and Herr, 1982).

If you're unsure about the safety of following your attorney's instructions not to answer a question, say you want the matter brought before the court. This may cause the opposition to withdraw or modify the objectionable question.

Moral: In general, there's little to gain by refusing to answer questions about the facts of the case. What you can do is to limit your remarks to the specific question asked: Don't give away new ideas or concepts by going beyond the answer to the question.

Questions are often asked repeatedly in the hope that you'll give additional information. This may be done when the plaintiff's attorney doesn't know what specific questions to ask you to get more information. Asking the same questions over and over is one form of "fishing expedition," a blind attempt to get you to tell more.

Conflict: If you give different answers to the same question, you'll be proved a liar. If you give exactly the same answer to questions asked several times, you may be accused of having been told what to say: You worked out the answers with the help of your attorney and memorized them. It's Catch 22: You can be made to look bad if your answers to repetitious questions are inconsistent or if they're too consistent. Try to find a median route.

When faced with the same question repeatedly, you may feel the natural desire to clarify the issue for the person questioning you. You might want to give further explanations of the patient's condition as you understood it, the reasons you thought your treatment was best at the time, the success you've had with similar cases in the past, and the unusual circumstances that prevented your treatment from working.

Don't give further explanations! The plaintiff's attorney will learn more about your thoughts and beliefs concerning the case. These will be written down in the transcript, and you'll have to swear to their accuracy. The opposition will know more about the defense you might use in court. Answering and explaining repetitious questions may bring up issues the plaintiff's attorney wasn't aware of.

If you *are* asked the same question repeatedly, ask your attorney to request that the person recording the deposition read your previous answer. Whether or not that is done, don't change your answer. This gives no new or contradictory information.

If you're not given the courtesy of being able to hear your previous answer and are forced to answer the question again, do so. But realize that you're being treated unfairly and an attempt is being made to trip you up.

Action: Make the fishing trip expensive and frustrating for the opposition. If agreeable to your attorney, each time a repetitious question is asked, go through the same process of asking for your previous answer to be read and saying that you have nothing new to add. Maybe you can make the process so painfully slow that the opposition will stop asking repetitive questions.

Your deposition may be reviewed by a judge, so use such delaying tactics only when you are clearly being treated unfairly. Consider just going along with the unfair treatment if you may later want to make a complaint to the court.

YOU NEED TO AVOID GENERALITIES

You have the right to be asked clear, specific questions. An extreme example of a question that's too broad is, "Tell me everything you remember about this patient." Just how vague or general a question has to be before it's objectionable isn't clearly or consistently defined. If a question is so general that you would be excused from answering it, your attorney should object to the question.

You can deal with the request to answer general, broad questions. Let the opposition know that you simply don't understand what is meant by the unreasonable phrase, "Tell me what you remember about." Ask the attorney if the physical examination is the item of interest. In this way your question can be limited, you won't bring up issues the opposition doesn't know about, and you won't later be accused of withholding information because your answer was incomplete.

If you're asked how a certain condition is treated in general, say there's no one answer unless the case is more clearly described. Make sure any description you comment on includes the extenuating circumstances that made your case so difficult. If this can't be done, your answers should clearly show that you're talking about a case that is different than your patient's.

Tip: Avoid using (and agreeing with statements that use) words such as "always," "never," or "invariably." You may be held to broad generalizations you never intended to make.

CONTROLLING YOUR BODY LANGUAGE

Plaintiff's attorneys have the legal power to use all sorts of tricky maneuvers to get more information from you. But one thing they can't do without your assistance is read your mind.

They can try, though, by observing your body language—by watching your facial expressions, your posture, the speed, pitch, loudness, and intensity of your voice, and many other nonverbal forms of communication. As physicians, we note nonverbal body language when evaluating patients. Yet even though we do a good job of reading nonverbals, we're usually unpracticed at controlling our own. After all, we're practiced in watching others.

Attorneys are trained to take advantage of your openness. By watching nonverbals, they'll learn what topics can be raised to upset you, to make you lose your temper at a critical time. When you become upset during a deposition, your powers of reasoning wane. Just as important, attorneys read nonverbals in an attempt to learn more about a case. They'll continue or come back to a line of questioning if it's clear that you're uncomfortable with the topic.

Moral: To convey as little information as possible to the opposition, gain control of your nonverbals through practice before your deposition. Watch yourself on videotape. Read about body language. During the deposition don't let the attorney learn what sorts of insults could make you lose your temper. Minimize facial expressions and practice self-control. If all this preparation seems like a drag, we've found that it's worth it in defending your malpractice case.

Your posture should be comfortable for you. A neutral body position is good: hands open and on the table, no fidgeting or doodling, knees slightly separated, a slight smile occasionally. You lean forward slightly when appropriate. Your tone of voice should remain neutral.

Even with practice, you'll probably not be able to completely hide your emotions during the deposition. So deliberately show greater signs of righteous indignation and concern when topics are brought up that are only a little upsetting. This tactic will make it more difficult for the attorney to figure out how to effectively insult and embarrass you and will keep you from inadvertently pointing out those topics you find most difficult to discuss.

Tip: You can gain time to relax during the deposition by using body language. To gain time for relaxing, stretch, look out the window, seem to be thinking hard. Don't do this with difficult questions; just when you need a break.

One physician who has testified at many depositions not only recognizes such body-language techniques, he uses them. He looks the interrogator straight in the face throughout the deposition. He occasionally glances at the court reporter's hands to be sure he's not speaking too quickly. He reports this technique has paid off.

In sum: The questioning attorney may obtain the kind of testimony he wants from you by being friendly, smiling, and taking a relaxed posture when you give helpful responses. But watch out: He may discourage unfavorable responses from you by staring, speaking in an angry voice, or moving uncomfortably close to you. Realize that such ploys exist and be looking for them.

BEING COMFORTABLE WITH SILENCE

A tactic used by attorneys to encourage physicians to go on talking and give too much information is to remain silent. There's a natural tendency to go on talking, especially if it seems that the person you're talking to expects you to say more. Say what's needed to honestly answer a question, and then shut up. Don't give lengthy (or any) explanations, apologies, comparisons, excuses, or commentary.

Moral: Accept periods of silence and be comfortable with them. Don't start talking when several opposition people lean toward you with expectant looks on their faces.

THE DIFFERENCE BETWEEN CLARIFICATION AND ELABORATION

When asked to explain a statement, be careful to clarify only what you've said. Don't elaborate. Elaboration involves adding details, giving new information, or making excuses for your past actions described by the statement.

While explanations may be desirable when testifying in front of a jury, there's no sense in trying to convince the plaintiff's attorney about anything. Just limit the amount of information he digs out of you.

WHEN YOU CAN'T REMEMBER CONVERSATIONS

It's recognized in law that it's difficult to remember the content of conversations in the distant past. While physicians often remember names, faces, and unusual or interesting medical findings, the details of conversations are usually forgotten.

In a deposition, you may be pushed to describe a conversation that occurred several years before. Don't respond to the natural desire to cooperate. The opposition may insinuate that what you do remember about the case is inaccurate because you can't recall a conversation (or other information).

Don't be intimidated. Be honest in telling what you do remember and don't fabricate or tell what you think might have been said. Before your deposition, try to make up your mind about what you do and don't remember.

Tip: When you do comment on a conversation, make it clear whether you're paraphrasing or quoting directly. Except for short phrases, most of what you say will usually be in the form of summarizing or paraphrasing.

DON'T SHOW ALL

As we've seen, the opposition can demand that you enter into evidence any notes you're carrying. Your deposition subpoena might have included a demand that you produce all papers, X-rays, and records of all kinds relevant to your case. So it's likely that any papers you take may be snatched up by the opposition. Attorneys have the right to examine the contents of the briefcase you carry with you to a deposition.

During your deposition, the plaintiff's attorney might ask if you have any correspondance or other materials that discuss the case. If you say Yes, he might extract a promise from you, under oath, to produce those letters and materials. Don't make such promises. Say that you want to review the materials with your attorney before you can say the material is discoverable.

Moral: Don't carry to the deposition descriptions of your strategy or anything else you don't want to show to the opposition. Don't promise to produce any other materials.

QUASH THE UNREASONABLE SUBPOENA

Your subpoena can order you to bring documents and other things to your deposition. A subpoena might ask you to bring unreasonable amounts or kinds of information. For example, it may ask for copies of the charts of the last hundred patients you saw who had chest pain. It would be difficult to find these, and an invasion of the privacy of your patients if you did bring them. Even if the charts could be obtained and the names omitted, the identities of many patients would still be clear, especially if you live in a small town.

Some courts have ruled that information about malpractice insurance policies isn't within the scope of proper deposition discovery.[1] That the existence of insurance can't be divulged in court, however, is well established. The existence and amount of insurance isn't relevant or material when deciding if negligence has occurred, but the amount of insurance coverage is discoverable in most jurisdictions. Information on your income or general financial condition generally won't be considered discoverable unless punitive damages are sought.

You may or may not have to tell the opposition how much insurance you have. On the other hand, many settlements are made for the amount the defendant's insurance will cover. You may want to tell how much insurance you have if such a settlement seems to be a possibility.

Though the validity of each of these objections can be debated, you can apply to the court for an order to modify or quash the subpoena. As stated in Rule 45 of the Federal Rules of Civil Procedure: "A subpoena may also command the person to whom it is directed to produce books, papers, documents, or tangible things designated therein; but the court, upon motion made promptly and in any event at or before the time specified in the subpoena for compliance therewith, may (1) quash or modify the subpoena if it is unreasonable and oppressive or (2) condition denial of the motion upon advancement by the person in whose behalf the subpoena is issued of the reasonable cost of producing the books, papers, documents, or tangible things."

AVOID DISCUSSING THE CASE INDISCRIMINANTLY

It's tempting to discuss your case before and after deposition with colleagues, nurses, friends, and family. Your words are bound to get back to someone who knows the plaintiff or the plaintiff's attorney. Like all rumors, the information will probably be distorted in the process. It's best not to talk.

On the days of the deposition itself when you discuss the case with your attorney, be sure you're out of earshot of the opposition. Some walls don't stop sound. The people in the elevator or at the next table in the restaurant may be relatives or friends of the plaintiff.

CONCLUSIONS

It's to your benefit to limit the flow of information to the opposition. Be comfortable with periods of silence, and don't elaborate unnecessarily. Don't bring material to the deposition that the opposition shouldn't see. Make sure no one can hear when you discuss the case with your attorney.

The next chapter describe ways in which information can be used against you long after it is obtained.

REFERENCES

1. Dolan, 1975 supplement.

12

DEPOSITION TRAPS THAT CATCH YOU LATER

There are important differences between medical and legal thinking that cause physicians to make statements that are time bombs. Though you may not realize it during the deposition, your statements and temper are being watched. When you make a wrong move, it's noted but not acknowledged. Later at the bargaining table or in court, your inaccurate statements will be brought up. When questioning you later in the deposition or in court, your temper will be made to flare just when you need the most concentration and composure.

WHEN MEDICAL AND LEGAL THINKING DIFFER

Physicians make damaging statements during depositions because they don't understand the legal logic that can prove the opposition's case. In medicine (or any physical science), a fact is discovered and proved by obtaining and considering *all* the available data; the one truth is found.

When considering a dispute in law, however, there are always two or more sides to an argument, each of which can be "proved" by considering the supporting data, relevant law, and previous legal case decisions. Each side in the dispute will argue for its conclusion, emphasizing different data about the case, different laws, and different legal case precedents.

In medicine or science, essentially everyone of adequate eduction considering the data will reach the same conclusion. In law, decisions made by several judges of the same court are often split nearly equally. Dissenting opinions are expected. Higher appellate courts disagree with lower appellate courts.

The differences in the way "facts are proved" in law can work against the physician in the deposition. Statements the physician makes that inadvertently help the opposition will be remembered and used; the deposition as a whole won't be considered in a balanced or complete manner. In the deposition the physician may feel he has explained his point of view and the facts of the case adequately. When repetitious questions are asked, for example, the physician may not feel the need to be complete or to qualify his answers each time they are given because the points have already been explained. This lack of persistence in being complete and detailed will give the plaintiff's attorney inaccurate statements. These statements can be taken out of context and later used to prove medically untrue points to the physician's detriment.

Playing with words: In addition to logic and thinking being different in law as opposed to medicine, the meaning of words is different. Consider the word "negligent." A physician gave his best effort for a difficult patient with multiple injuries and had a better result than most physicians in a similar situation would have had. Nevertheless, one injury was overlooked, leading to a permanent impairment; the physician was too busy with resuscitation to do a detailed examination of every extremity. Many physicians wouldn't consider the patient's treatment negligent. However, legal reasoning might prove that a careful examination would have avoided the permanent impairment.

Words such as "authoritative," and "expert" have been discussed in this book. The physician should be familiar with the various—and subjective—meanings of such terms before giving a deposition. Because of the way legal "logic" works, the physician must make every statement in the deposition accurate, complete, and not potentially injurious to his case.

Moral: Medical and legal thinking, as well as the definitions of words, are different. Realize that you are in foreign territory.

STATING YOUR FEELINGS ABOUT PATIENTS: THE RISKS

You're jumping into a deep trap when you answer questions concerning your feelings about the plaintiff. The opposition is looking for a motive for your alleged carelessness and indifference toward the patient. If you say anything at all negative, this can later be repeated—distorted—to a jury. "Dr. Jones said he thought the patient was irresponsible and never paid his bills. The doctor disliked the patient from the start. That's why he wouldn't come to check his chest pain in the middle of the night."

Examples: If asked about the plaintiff's bill-paying record, say you don't remember it very well, but you can look it up. If asked about your feelings, opinions, or attitudes about the plaintiff, say something truthful but positive. The plaintiff may have beaten his children and never paid his bills, but maybe you could say he was pleasant to talk to. If you say anything negative, the jury will hear about it in the worst context.

THE OPPOSITION WILL FIND YOUR TRIGGER POINTS

The plaintiff's attorney is sure to find out how to get you angry or frustrated. It may be that you flare up if your authority or skill are questioned in a sarcastic manner. You may not do well answering many basic questions about the case; you may get impatient and be manipulated into making explanations so simple that they're inaccurate.

Once the opposition finds out how to get you upset, this information can be used against you immediately, as well as years later at your trial. You can be driven to the point of poor concentration during your deposition and then asked about an important issue. If you answer ineffectively, you will no longer be regarded as a person who can remain in control in times of stress. A trial jury might well conclude this is why your patient didn't do well.

To avoid exposing your trigger points, learn to control your temper and concentrate on handling yourself level-headedly. Also, as discussed earlier, learn to control your body language. Show some of your emotions, but only at times when you're not that concerned about them. In this way, if the attorney chooses to bully you, he won't know what issues truly get you mad. If the bullying continues beyond reason during the deposition, it can serve as a basis for proving harrassment.

INACCURATE STATEMENTS WILL HAUNT YOU LATER

Take time to think of what you say. Ask your attorney to note any inaccurate statements you might make during the deposition. Then when reviewing and signing the deposition transcript, make corrections as needed. If inaccurate statements aren't corrected, the opposition will note them when reviewing the transcript. Inaccurate statements can be brought up at the bargaining table and in court. It then becomes more difficult to make corrections.

Caution: Too many physicians become hot under the collar when corrected. Their egos are amazing. For example, many physicians won't listen to a coronary-care nurse who suggests a drug to treat a cardiac arrhythmia. The fact is that these nurses treat such arrhythmias every day of the week and know what to do. So let your attorney know before the deposition that you'll not become irritated if corrected or asked to reconsider your answer.

FEELING THE PLAINTIFF'S ATTORNEY'S WHIP

If an answer given later in the deposition or in court isn't consistent with an earlier answer, you'll be "proved" a liar. Your testimony will be impeached or shown to be invalid. Though the slip-up may occur on a minor point you were just speculating on, the inconsistency can be damaging at the settlement table and impressive to a jury. So never guess, estimate, or speculate about anything; just tell what you know for sure.

Fancy opposition tactics: The use of deposition testimony during a trial is described in a legal journal:[1] "To impeach or contradict the adverse trial witness with prior deposition testimony, counsel will want to use the deposition. . .much as a lion tamer uses a whip and chair. Every time that adverse witness strays from his deposition-. . .let him feel the whip. . .by confronting him with the former testimony to impeach his credibility and force out crucial admissions."

One often-used technique of presenting deposition testimony to a jury is for the plaintiff's attorney to read the deposition questions and have another attorney read the physician's answers. Great efforts are sometimes made to select and prepare the person who reads the physician's deposition answers to give the most dramatic effect.

The presentation may be slanted because statements are taken out of context. If so, insist that material before and after the section selected for presentation to the jury by the opposition is also presented. A long reading from the deposition transcript and a comprehensive narrative explanation of the situation may bore the jury and dilute the point the opposition is trying to make, but you do have the right to a balanced presentation of your testimony.

Lesson: Know the deposition transcript well so that you'll not be forced to "feel the whip."

WHEN THE ANSWERS CHANGE OVER TIME

Don't fall into the trap of giving information that's inaccurate because the information is dated.

Example: During discussions about the proper treatment in your case, if a medical reference were written after your case occurred, make this fact clear in your deposition transcript. It's recognized in law that you don't have the ability to predict future developments in medicine! Certainly, medications and acceptable medical practice change all the time.

It may be that the policies and procedures of the hospital you work in influenced the care of the patient. If they're used as evidence in your suit, be sure that policy and procedure manuals are correct for the date of the case. These items are revised irregularly. Your insurance carrier should be willing to pay for finding and duplicating these manuals. But even so, it may be necessary to subpoena records from your own hospital so that people with access to these records will make the effort to get the material together.

Another factor that you may be questioned about later is *damages* to the plaintiff. Chances are you've not seen, much less examined or taken care of, the plaintiff for years. Limit your descriptions of damages to what you really know firsthand. Don't make guesses about probable long-term pain or suffering. Don't speculate about disability: We've all seen blind and other severely handicapped people function well economically and in other ways.

In avoiding future disasters, be especially careful not to refer to the plaintiff as having low pain tolerance or being irresponsible or lazy. Labels you apply will be taken out of context and used at the bargaining table or in front of the jury to prove that you had a dislike for or prejudice against the patient. Limit your comments to observable, objective facts: the patient was unemployed, had a high blood alcohol level, repeatedly lost prescriptions, and so on.

CONCLUSIONS

Medical and legal thinking are vastly different, facts are proved differently in law than in science or medicine. Words have different meanings. Many physicians don't realize they're fighting in foreign territory and fall into hidden traps. The results of such falls may be felt years later when the case is settled or goes to court.

Avoiding deposition traps requires repeated practice. The next chapter tells you how.

REFERENCES

1. Blumenkopf JS: *Deposition Strategy and Tactics.* The American Journal of Trial Advocacy 1981;5:231-251.

13

IF YOU DON'T REHEARSE, YOU'LL GOOF

One physician with many years of experience as a legal consultant and expert witness has said: "If I practice for a deposition, I do well. If I don't rehearse ahead of time, I simply goof."

The physician is a good speaker who's extremely good at thinking on his feet while practicing medicine. He's testified in many depositions. Yet he's found through experience that certain steps must be taken before each deposition if a favorable outcome is forthcoming. These steps, which you *must* take, are described in this chapter.

HOW TO BECOME SKILLED AT ANSWERING DEPOSITION QUESTIONS

1. Set aside time for rehearsing your deposition over several months. You must become practiced in using all the information in this book with little conscious effort.
2. Coordinate your rehearsal efforts with your attorney.
3. Practice answering questions—especially those listed in chapters 6 and 8. Also practice on questions relevant to your case that make use of the confusion-causing techniques and tactics of psychological warfare described in previous chapters.
4. Give repeated attention to difficult questions.

5. Rehearse until you're comfortable and the techniques of answering are automatic and familiar to you.

6. Work on self-image, relaxation, and handling difficult situations.

APPLYING THE LESSONS OF THIS BOOK

During a deposition, you can't take time to stop and think of how each question might contain a trap. When asked a question, there's not enough time for you to stop and think, "What did that book say about authoritative references?" or "Do I really have to answer with just a Yes or No?"

To effectively apply the information in this book, you must practice in the systematic and determined manner described below. You're capable of this, or you would never have made it through medical school. Years of training, practice, and experience have given you the ability to react "without thinking." You don't need to fumble for a diagnosis and treatment or the words to describe them because you're practiced in handling medical situations. If you're uneasy with a situation and can't make a diagnosis, you call a consultant. So give your deposition the kind of practice and preparation that can make most of it routine and comfortable for you. This means that you must go through the entire deposition several times in your own mind. To the extent possible, there must be no surprise questions.

DON'T ENLIST YOUR SPOUSE

While preparing for your deposition, another person can ask you questions and help judge your responses. Don't make that person your spouse, unless he or she is a physician or nurse and is also being sued in the same case.

Though she may volunteer to help, the case will eventually take enough of her time to be a frustration. Don't add to it. Taking part in practice questioning would add to her tension: Detailed knowledge about the case would give her more things to worry about.

PREPARING FOR THE DEPOSITION: WHERE DOES THE TIME COME FROM?

Make it a point to avoid non-productive discussions with your spouse and friends. Instead, spend time preparing for the deposition.

If your deposition is a year away, you might want to spend just a few hours a month on it. As the deposition grows near, you'll need to spend one, and finally several, hours a week on it. Schedule the rehearsal sessions for when you're reasonably fresh. Don't let the rehearsal sessions interfere with your family life or activities that are important to you. It's better to cancel a few office hours than to leave your spouse alone with the kids.

Tip: If you're ordered to defend yourself in a deposition on short notice, say you won't have time to review the case until a later date. If that fails, stay in bed and call in sick if you have to, but don't go unprepared.

There are several reasons to prepare for your deposition over months. You'll look for the information or run across it in the medical literature over time. Your hospital librarian can do computer searches of the literature and get articles for you on a few weeks notice—a great time-saver.

Issues and questions will come up that you won't know how to deal with initially. You'll find the answers by discussing the theoretical or medical issues (without mentioning the case) with other physicians, speaking to your attorney, and thinking about the issues over time.

PRACTICING—STEP BY STEP

Let's assume that you've learned the facts of your case, the relevant medical literature, and the information contained in this book. Then proceed along these lines:

- Read the practice questions given in the early chapters, modifying them to make them relevant to your case. State the answers out loud, as if you were at a deposition. At first you may be slow, looking for the trap in each question and trying to avoid falling into it. You may need to refer to the medical chart, an anatomy book, or this book to help you answer some questions.

- When you're comfortable with the sample questions in this book, make up difficult questions of your own. Pretend you're the patient's attorney, hoping to make $1,000,000 from the case. Make up leading, nasty, unfair, and ambiguous questions. When waiting in lines, doing housework, getting dressed, or taking a walk alone, go over deposition questions and answers that are difficult.

- During some of your practice sessions, recite the questions into a tape recorder. Play one question at a time and stop the tape while you give your answer. Imagine that several obnoxious attorneys are staring at you and appearing not to accept your explanations. Imagine the attorney and other persons at the deposition looking displeased at your answers.

- Don't memorize answers to questions. The form of questions will be different than you expect. Practice answering in a spontaneous, comfortable manner. Once you're familiar with the case and have practiced answering questions enough, you'll acquire the ability to answer easily and spontaneously.

- Occasionally use a second tape recorder (audio or preferably video) to monitor your performance. Review the tape critically. How much you should monitor depends on how satisfied you are with your performance. Erase all question-and-answer tapes before your actual deposition. They're "discoverable."

After many sessions of practice questioning, you'll become relatively comfortable and confident. You'll have the energy necessary to concentrate on the truly difficult and unusual questions.

- Once you're satisfied with your performance, have your attorney quiz you. Pretend that the deposition is really taking place; simulate every detail as much as possible. Wear your dress suit. Use an uncomfortable chair, make the room temperature too hot, imagine that the patient with his wife and attorney are frowning at your answers.

Your practice with your attorney is privilegd; it can't be discussed at your deposition. If he doesn't have the time to cooperate with such preparation, get another attorney into the case to help you with your deposition practice, or replace your attorney entirely.

TAKE A CRAM COURSE SHORTLY BEFORE THE DEPOSITION?

Don't do it. As you mull over difficult questions and explanations for what happened in your malpractice case month after month, new insights and explanations will come to you. Giving your mind time to process information in this manner is one reason to avoid counting on a cram course just before your deposition. Even if you know all about your case and have memorized this book, you're sure to fumble at answering questions if you haven't practiced over a period of time.

REHEARSING YOUR SELF-IMAGE

Your practiced self-image during deposition must be one of dignity, honesty, confidence, and strength. To maintain dignity you must be able to handle insults. Think up a variety of upsetting questions and statements that the patient's attorney might throw at you. Attorney intimidation and provocation were discussed earlier. Mix these upsetting questions in with your other questions in all your rehearsal sessions. Realize how these statements might make you angry: Your pulse and blood pressure rise, you turn red and clench your fist.

Practice relaxation: At first, it will take you ten minutes or more to relax each part of your body systematically. With practice you will be able to go into the relaxed state in a second. When an upsetting question comes your way, you'll be able to quickly reverse the physiological and psychological upsets within seconds. With practice, you'll learn to begin the relaxation process before you even begin to become tense. *Then you'll be in control of yourself and of the deposition.*

Once you've acquired the ability to relax, do it while thinking of the worst insults and intimidations the opposition could throw at you. Imagine yourself in the deposition being embarrassed, and relax. Practice being relaxed under the most adverse conditions.

Polishing your image: Your ability to defend yourself is limited by your self-image. After you've rehearsed a lot, you may find that you're still frightened about the prospect of being questioned for hours by an experienced attorney. It takes about a month for most people to change their self-image. You may have to change from a frightened, picked-on person to an aggressive fighter. You must stop seeing yourself as being less clever than an attorney. You must work on your self-image daily for at least a month. Here are some tips:

1. If you're not confident about any potential questions or issues, discuss them with your attorney and depose yourself repeatedly until you're sure of how you would deal with the problems.
2. Read and analyze depositions of recent malpractice cases in your area, if possible ones conducted by the attorneys you'll be facing. Your attorney can get them for you.
3. Picture yourself doing well in the deposition. Think positively about your ability to handle the many techniques used to trick physicians.
4. Rehearse in your mind how you would handle various insults. By the time the insults occur, you'll be relaxed and used to them. And you'll respond to them in ways you decided on after

much consideration. You might simply say, "I don't like such outrageous insults." Having the word "outrageous" in the deposition transcript can help form the foundation for a countersuit (see "Outrage" in Glossary).

5. Set aside ten minutes a day for thinking about your self-image. Turn ideas of persecution into the realization that you're one of the many successful people who are being sued.

6. Instead of letting anxiety steal time from your family, make it a point to spend more time with your wife and children (but don't spend the time discussing the case). Increase (or start) your exercise program.

CONCLUSIONS

The unpleasant message is that you must actually *practice* for your deposition using the information contained in this book. Only with such practice will you become more confident, skilled, and effective than the lawyer who's suing you.

Much of what you and your attorney say and do during depositions can lay the foundation for a countersuit. You must make sure that certain facts come out in your and other peoples' depositions. The next chapter will familiarize you with the types of countersuits and tell how you might make use of them.

REFERENCES

1. Maltz M: *Psychocybernetics.* New York, Simon & Schuster, 1960.

14

MAKE DEPOSITIONS DOCUMENT THE EVIDENCE NEEDED FOR A COUNTERSUIT

Once your case is settled, don't think that you're safe. You're in the midst of a crisis. American physicians paid more than $2 billion in 1984 for malpractice insurance, yet to cover their claims the carriers needed still more. General surgeons on Long Island, N.Y., for example, pay more than $47,000 a year for $1,000,000/$3,000,000 occurrence policies. Additional surcharges are levied against physicians who have been sued before.[1]

One of the reasons for the present crisis is that physicians haven't filed countersuits when they were justified. Countersuits can do more than discourage frivolous lawsuits. They can decrease (or obtain compensation for) abusive, outrageous, and upsetting treatment that physicians sometimes receive during a lawsuit that isn't frivolous. Such unreasonable behavior not only upsets the physician, it may increase the settlement amount unreasonably by distorting the facts of the case.

Countersuit from a deposition? Yes, indeed. Depositions can lay the foundation for a countersuit. There are several types of malpractice countersuits that can be supported by the evidence contained in depositions. You may be able to countersue even if your case doesn't go to trial.

A traditional countersuit is a lawsuit charging malicious prosecution. In fact, there are a number of different reasons, or "legal theories," that can be used as a basis to sue the plaintiff and his attorney. These include malicious prosecution, suing without the plaintiff's permission, defamation (libel or slander), abuse of process, prima facie tort, invasion of privacy, infliction of emotional distress, and conflict of interest.[2]

Though you must initiate the lawsuit, an attorney will be needed to help you file it and carry it out. Malpractice insurance companies are likely to support the filing of such suits because they've been demonstrated to reduce the number of malpractice claims filed.

Example: In the 18 months following the landmark Leonard Berlin malpractice countersuit case, the number of malpractice suits filed against doctors in the greater Chicago area was down 42 percent, even though Dr. Berlin lost his countersuit. In the suits that did occur after the Berlin case, fewer doctor co-defendants were named. In 1975 in Cook County, Ill., the total number of physicians named as defendants in malpractice suits was 1,499. In 1977, the number was only 628, a reduction of 58 percent.[3]

In a meaningful way, Dr. Berlin clearly "won" his countersuit.

A BOOST FOR COUNTERSUITS

Medical practice as we know it may soon end unless the number of malpractice suits is decreased. Already $2 billion a year is paid in awards to malpractice patients and their attorneys. Many physicians have gone out of practice or moved to states with lower insurance rates. Others have eliminated high-risk procedures from their practices. As we know, many board-certified obstetricians no longer deliver babies.

Lawyers have learned that they can file a frivolous malpractice suit and collect a few thousand dollars in settlement. This is true because it's easier for the physician and less expensive for his insurance company to settle than to take the case to court.

Why physicians settle: They're afraid of *not* settling out of court. Too often juries will take the attitude that sick or injured patients need money to live on, and there's nothing wrong with taking it from the rich doctor or insurance company even if the physician gave competent care.

Various kinds of legislation, arbitration boards, and other measures have been tried. Some legislation, such as that limiting the awards for pain and suffering or that spreads payments out over time, may help discourage lawsuits.

COUNTERSUITS: A SIGNIFICANT CHALLENGE

One measure that will reduce the number of malpractice suits is the filing of a countersuit whenever an unwarranted malpractice suit occurs. Even if the countersuit isn't won, it will be successful in discouraging further groundless suits. Every countersuit filed against a frivolous suit will succeed in teaching the attorney involved (and others who hear about it) that a nuisance suit settled for several thousand dollars will end up costing the plaintiff and his attorney plenty by the time they finish defending your countersuit.

Countersuits are more easily won if the malpractice case is decided in your favor. But that's not always necessary. Case precedents and laws have been changing recently, and they give attorneys a responsibility to the people they sue. Attorneys are now obligated in many jurisdictions to investigate lawsuits before they're filed to see if there are grounds for a lawsuit.

Moral: This change in the law will reduce the number of frivolous malpractice suits—if physicians countersue in appropriate cases.

COUNTERSUITS: SOME DRAWBACKS

Physicians have been discouraged from filing countersuits because they're usually ruled against in the courts. But you should take the attitude that a countersuit has succeeded if the suit even temporarily discourages frivolous malpractice suits in one's town or costs the attorney and plaintiff as much as they won when they sued you. Defending countersuits costs money.

In the past, insurance companies haven't paid for the court costs and lawyers' fees associated with countersuits. Possibly because the cases have been so unsuccessful, lawyers usually won't take a case on a contigent-fee basis.

HOW THE DEPOSITION TRANSCRIPT CAN DOCUMENT WRONGDOING

Even though countersuits have had limited success, consider them. The transcript of your deposition will document unfair questioning tactics of the opposing attorney. Any malicious or emotionally distressing treatment you receive during your deposition will be documented in the transcript if the suggestions given in previous chapters are followed.

If there's no foundation for the malpractice claims against you, all the depositions taken for the case will document the lack of grounds for the malprctice suit. Your patient's deposition may document the fact that he didn't want to sue you or that claims of damages have been exaggerated by his attorney.

Questions asked of various witnesses, including the patient, might show that the patient didn't cooperate with treatment. Given the fact that the patient and his attorney know this, you might be able to countersue because they're blaming you for something you're obviously not responsible for.

Tip: Give your attorney lists of questions to ask each witness. Tell him the reasons for the questions. Such questions might include the following:

Questions for the plaintiff:

1. I note that your wife continued to see Dr. Cutter after your unsuccessful surgery. If you felt he does such bad work, why did your wife persist in seeing him?
2. I note that you describe in great detail events that occurred during the time your blood alcohol was twice the legally intoxicated level. Is your memory really that good when you're drunk, or did someone else tell you what happened? Could we get your blood alcohol level as high as it was and test your memory?
3. I note that you didn't keep your appointments as recommended. Do you think the doctor might have discovered that you were having problems and could have done something about it, had he seen you?
4. Your income tax and pharmacy records indicate that you didn't take the prescribed medicine. Could you explain this?

Questions for the plaintiff and the plaintiff's spouse separately:

1. What complications did Dr. Cutter say might result from the surgery?
2. Did you think that the surgery would be completely safe and have no complications?
3. Do you really think that any surgery is completely safe?

WHAT PLAINTIFF'S ATTORNEYS ARE GETTING AWAY WITH

As stated in the New York University Law Review, "Attorneys generally owe a duty of care solely to their clients, and courts therefore seldom hold them liable for negligence resulting in injury to third parties. ... Third-party plaintiffs have been denied compensation, and attorney misconduct has not been deterred. ... Clients may not have sufficient interest to bring suit—they may be untouched by the attorney's conduct, they may be bankrupt, or they may even have benefitted from the attorney's negligence.[4]

This situation is changing. Federal laws and some state courts have begun to recognize the duty of attorneys to investigate the reasonableness of lawsuits before they're filed.

Your relationship to the patient's attorney: It's simple. He's knowledgeable about the law and is trying to use it to get your money. He's not trying to improve the quality of medicine. Malpractice lawsuits demand payment when treatment was not, in retrospect, complete, accurate, and optimum. Meticulous care, regardless of cost or probability of success, must be given in every case.

For example, studies have shown that lumbar spine X-rays aren't cost effective in patients with "lumbar strain" unless there has been major trauma. Yet, if an unsuspected tumor wasn't detected because X-rays weren't taken, the lawsuit resulting might result in more money damages than all the thousands of negative X-ray costs.

Lesson: The cost effectiveness of medical practice is now being defined in terms of the cost of a lawsuit raised if a rare finding isn't detected.

A drunk driver not wearing a seat belt who can't describe his symptoms because of intoxication will sue a physician for not detecting his injuries. And a lawyer is there to help him sue the physician. This is outrageous! Make sure the depositions taken of all parties document such information so that a countersuit for malicious prosecution, outrageous treatment, or other type of countersuit described below can succeed.

USE COUNTERSUITS ONLY WHEN INDICATED

Initiate a countersuit when it's clear that your malpractice suit was unfounded, or when the treatment you received during the lawsuit was unreasonable. If you can understand why the malpractice suit was justified and it was conducted in a reasonable manner, a countersuit isn't justified.

Reminder: Countersuing is a difficult project that should be undertaken only after much consideration. It costs time and money. There are few precedents of successful countersuits.

HOW YOUR DEPOSITION CAN SUPPORT A MALICIOUS-PROSECUTION COUNTERSUIT

Though it's received much publicity, the malpractice countersuit has proved difficult to win. The term "countersuit" is technically reserved for a malicious-prosecution suit in which malicious intent must be proved. *It's necessary to have won the malpractice case before the suit can be initiated.* So if unfair legal practices help the plaintiff win a suit against you, countersuit isn't possible.

This Catch-22 situation doesn't exist when suing under other legal theories. For example, you can claim you were defamed whether or not you won the suit.

Every malpractice suit will insult and upset the physician involved. Some amount of unfairness must be endured without complaint so that justice can be done in unclear cases. Earlier we've seen how to make the deposition transcript document unreasonable amounts of intimidation and other malicious behavior that might occur during a deposition.

In sum: The deposition transcripts of all persons involved in a lawsuit will be the chief source of proof for a countersuit, unless the case is one of the few malpractice cases that go to court.

Note in the accompanying box that if you lose your case, you can't claim malicious prosecution. If your case is settled for some amount of money, it probably won't be possible to claim malicious prosecution. But if the suit is dismissed or abandoned, a malicious-prosecution suit will be possible. However, dismissal on technicalities such as the statute of limitations may not suffice. State laws differ on whether a malicious-prosecution suit can be filed before the original suit against the physician has been settled.

The definition of malice differs from state to state. It may be defined as reckless disregard for the truth, motivation by ill-will, or forcing a settlement without a reasonable belief that the suit has merit. Malice is easiest to prove when there's evidence of intent to injure or annoy the physician. It's possible to argue that malice existed because of proven anger provoked by aggressive attempts to collect bills or impersonal care.

States disagree on what constitutes damages. Claimed damages

BOX 14-1

Necessary Elements of a Malicious-Prosecution Suit

> 1. A judicial proceeding has been initiated or continued by the plaintiff against the physician.
> 2. The physician prevailed in this proceeding.
> 3. There was no probable cause to institute the proceeding.
> 4. The proceeding was instituted because of malice.
> 5. The physician sustained injury.

include defamation of character and reputation, mental distress, time away from practice, increased malpractice insurance rates, and attorney's fees, and in some states they're not acceptable as factors in a countersuit.

Lesson: This reasoning seems to imply that because all physicians being sued suffer these losses, they have nothing to complain about! It's becoming accepted that courts have a general disdain for malicious-prosecution suits.

A CASE HISTORY

The Court of Appeals of Tennessee upheld a jury award of $11,500 to a physician whose countersuit against his patient and her attorney was based on malicious prosecution and abuse of process.[5] In this case, the patient was told she might have gonorrhea and that laboratory tests would be needed to confirm this. She was properly treated. A week later she returned to the physician and found she had not had gonorrhea. A year later she filed a suit claiming that the physician was negligent in diagnosing gonorrhea because he took tests that took unnecessarily long to yield results. It was also claimed that the physician was receiving kickbacks from the laboratory.

It was determined that the patient didn't receive culture results promptly because she hadn't called the office as instructed. Yet she claimed that the delay in finding out whether or not she had gonorrhea was due to the negligence of the physician.

The patient claimed that the delay caused her great anxiety and mental anguish; she sought $100,000 in compensatory and punitive damages. The claim that the physician was receiving kickbacks was suggested by the patient's attorney and had no basis in fact. He claimed that the Rules of Civil Procedure permit making any allegation that comes to mind even though there is no basis for it, with the idea of proving or disproving the allegation at some later date. The attorney had been a laboratory technician in the past and had known of two physicians who split fees with laboratories. Based on that he claimed that this physician was receiving kickbacks. The attorney made essentially no efforts to investigate the case. He lost it and appealed. The attorney carried on a groundless appeal without the consent of his client and eventually had to pay the physician damages on the basis of malicious prosecution and abuse of process.

HOW THE LAW IS CHANGING

In a recent case the Kansas Supreme Court determined that an attorney must conduct a reasonable investigation to find the true facts of a case before filing a civil action on behalf of his client (Nelson v. Miller, et al 227 Kan 271 p.2d 1980). According to this decision, when determining if an attorney had malice when filing a lawsuit, a jury may consider that the attorney had a duty to investigate.[6] Such court decisions (and Rule 11 of the Federal Rules of Civil Procedure, as revised in 1983), give attorneys the responsibility of investigating cases before they're filed.

CONCLUSIONS

Countersuits can be initiated in response to unfair treatment as well as for frivolous claims. Countersuits should encourage attorneys to deal with physicians in a more reasonable manner, seek only justifiable damages, and file fewer frivolous claims. Keep the possibility of a countersuit in mind when giving your deposition and planning the depositions of others with your attorney.

REFERENCES

1. Crane M: Malpractice: Will the new premium hikes pull you under?. *Medical Economics* 1985;May 27.

2. Duke NS: Causes of attorney malpractice claims 3, Professional Liability Reporter 199, 1979, in Pfennigstorf W: *Types and causes of lawyers' professional liability claims: The search for facts.* Spring 1980, vol 253, pp 255-302, American Bar Foundation Research Journal; also Rothblat HB: *Handling health practitioner cases,* chapter 28: Physicians Countersuits and Defamation, pp 407-423, The Lawyers Co-Operative Publishing Co, Rochester, New York, and Bancroft-Whitney Co., San Francisco, Calif., 1983.

3. Berlin L: Countersuit pp 117-133, in James EJ: *Legal Medicine With Special Reference to Diagnostic Imaging.* Urban & Schwartzenberg, Baltimore-Munich, 1980.

4. Eisenberg ES: *Attorneys' negligence and third parties.* New York University Law Review, vol 57:126, pp 126-163, April, 1982.

5. Taub S: Malpractice countersuits: Succeeding at last? *Law, Medicine & Health Care,* December 1981.

6. Goldman JK: *Lawyer beware! New development in attorneys' liability.* Journal of the Kansas Bar Association, pp 88-96, Summer, 1981.

GLOSSARY

Further information can be obtained from legal dictionaries, such as Black's Law Dictionary, from which some of these definitions were derived in part.

ADMISSIBLE EVIDENCE. Evidence that can be introduced in court. In federal courts, admissibility of evidence is governed by the Federal Rules of Evidence. Information that would not be admissible in court can be investigated in a deposition.

ARBITRATION. The settlement of a dispute by an impartial third party.

ARGUMENTATIVE QUESTION. A question that debates a previously given answer more than once or twice.

AUTHORITATIVE. Conclusive, unquestioned. To say that a book or article is authoritative is to say that statements made in the work are accurate. To say that an author is authoritative is to say that you swear everything he has said or written is true. Of course, no book, article, or person is forever up to date or completely accurate. So the physician falls into a trap when he agrees that a work or author is authoritative. A physician who says that his knowledge was based on any certain book or article will be embarrassed when an innaccuracy is found in the work.

BADGER. To harrass or torment.

BIAS. The predisposition to decide an issue in a certain way.

BODY LANGUAGE. See *Nonverbals*.

CIVIL. Relating to private rights. A civil wrong, or tort, is a wrong against another individual. A criminal wrong is an act against the state. Murder, assault, and battery can be prosecuted as criminal as well as civil wrongs. Some malpractice insurance policies don't cover criminal acts. A physician might be charged with a criminal act simply because the statute of limitations has run for the relevant civil proceedings.

COMMON LAW. Statutory law refers to laws passed by the legislature. But because the legislature can't think of everything that might ever happen, courts have to decide right and wrong every time a law doesn't exactly fit. The collection of court decisions establish case law, also called common law. Case decisions in one state are not necessarily followed in other states. Case decisions in lower courts have less weight than decisions of higher courts. Decisions in courts lower than an appellate court carry very little weight. State courts don't always follow federal decisions or laws. Appellate courts, even in the same state, often disagree when deciding an issue.

CONFIDENTIAL. Intended to be kept secret. A confidential relationship, also called a fiduciary relationship, is one in which communications are expected to be kept secret. See also *Privilege*.

CONFLICT OF INTEREST. A situation in which a person owes allegiance to two parties with differing needs. For example, the attorney furnished by your malpractice insurance company may have the company tell him to settle the case when you don't want to settle.

COMPARATIVE NEGLIGENCE. See *Contributory Negligence* and *Negligence*.

CONTRIBUTORY NEGLIGENCE. This means that the patient contributed through his own action (or inaction) to his injury. Comparative negligence is a type of contributory negligence, not recognized in all states, in which negligence is measured in terms of percentage. Thus, a patient with a million dollars worth of damages who was 30 percent responsible for the damages might claim his physician owed him $700,000. See also *Negligence*.

COUNTERSUIT. Suing the person(s) who sued you. Classically, the word "countersuit" refers to a malicious-prosecution countersuit. However, there are a number of other types of countersuits that can be supported by the evidence contained in depositions.

CRIME. See *Civil*.

CROSS-EXAMINATION. The questioning of a witness in a deposition, trial, or hearing. The material covered in cross-examination is technically limited to subjects covered in initial (direct) questioning. However, in depositions, the subject matter covered is usually not limited. Direct and cross-examination are often mixed, and there is little limitation of the scope of questioning.

DAMAGE. Personal or property loss. Or injury caused by accident, negligence, or the intentional act of another person. In a malpractice case, an attempt is made to "make the person whole," to undo the damages, by means of a cash settlement. If a jury feels that the malpractice was done in a deliberate, criminal, indifferent, or grossly negligent manner, additional damages may be awarded. These additional damages may be called exemplary, punitive, or vindictive damages. Some malpractice policies won't cover such additional damages.

The physician being sued might suffer damages because of the lawsuit. He might countersue, asking for recovery for his damages. See *Special Damages* and *Special Injury.*

DEEP POCKET. A physician or other person with a bank account healthy enough to make it worth an attorney's time to go after him.

DEFAMATION. Defamation is action that causes damage to another's reputation. Criminal as well as civil charges of defamation can be made. Physicians have to put up with publication of damaging statements because some papers filed with a court can legally be published. However, statements made to the press about a malpractice case by the patient or his attorney should be carefully studied for defamatory material. Such statements could provide the basis for a lawsuit for defamation. See also *Slander, Libel.*

DEPONENT. A deponent is one who testifies in a deposition. The person being questioned.

DEPOSE. Cause to give information in the form of a deposition.

DEPOSITION. A meeting of the parties involved in a lawsuit, their attorneys, a reporter, and possibly other persons. Sworn testimony is taken and recorded word for word by a notary or other officer authorized to administer oaths. The testimony may be used in court.

DEPOSITION TRANSCRIPT. The written record of the deposition, a word-for-word account of what is said during a deposition. Nonverbal actions may also be recorded. The deposition transcript is a legal document that can be quoted in court. Attorneys frequently study, index, and cross-reference deposition transcripts. The deposition transcript is proof of any admissions a defendant might make during hours of long questioning.

DISCOVERABLE. Information is discoverable if it's suitable for examination during a deposition. Any information that might be expected to lead to facts relevant to the case in question is discoverable. Much information that wouldn't be admissible in court will be discoverable.

DISCOVERY. Finding the facts of a case. Discovery includes studying medical records and obtaining information by means of depositions.

DISCOVERY RULE.   A rule, operative in some states, that the statute of limitations begins to run when the injury is recognized (or at the time when a reasonably diligent patient should have been ability to notice the injury).

EVASIVE ANSWER.   An answer that doesn't admit to or deny a fact in a direct manner. Rule 37 of the Federal Rules of Civil Procedure treats an evasive answer as a failure to answer. It provides a mechanism for obtaining a court order that demands the question be answered.

EVIDENCE.   It consists of testimony, records, and other things that can be used to prove the truth of a fact. See *In Evidence*.

EXAMINATION BEFORE TRIAL, OR EBT.   A deposition.

EXCULPATORY.   Excusing from guilt or fault. Exculpatory clauses in treatment consent forms, which hold health care personnel free of liability for negligence, are generally held to be invalid.

EXHIBIT.   A document or an object that can be examined. Exhibits used in medical malpractice cases include medical records, X-rays, and anatomical models.

EXPERT.   An expert is a person with specialized knowledge of a certain field. In general, the expert might have gained his or her knowledge through education or experience. However, in medical malpractice litigation, some courts have ruled that a physician isn't expert unless his knowledge has been gained through (or at least verified by) practical experience. See *Expert Witness*.

EXPERT WITNESS.   An expert (see above) who testifies at depositions and in court concerning medical facts relevant to a case. The expert can do much to help the defendant physician prepare for his own deposition. See *Independent Expert Witness*.

FEDERAL RULES OF CIVIL PROCEDURE.   A body of rules that governs all civil actions in United States District Courts. Most states model their rules of civil procedure on the Federal Rules.

FRAUD.   An intentional lie that has the purpose of causing another to part with a valuable or to give up a legal right. Fraudulent acts would probably be considered criminal acts and wouldn't be covered by most malpractice insurance policies. Fraud can extend the statute of limitations. For example, continuing to tell a patient that an unusual, permanent postoperative complication is normal and will spontaneously clear up would probably allow the patient to sue later than if the complication had been immediately acknowledged.

FRIVOLOUS.   Not at all supported by evidence. Lawsuits can be proved to be frivolous by depositions taken of various parties, such as the patient. The information obtained during such depositions can make a countersuit possible.

GOOD FAITH.　An abstract quality with no technical meaning or statutory definition. An honest belief and intention. Good-faith settlements may not be final: When the opposition claims it has "new" evidence about your case, they may ask you to pay more depending on terms of your "good faith settlement."

GROSS NEGLIGENCE.　The intentional failure to perform a duty in reckless disregard of the consequences to others. See also *Negligence*.

HARASSMENT.　Words, gestures, or actions that annoy, alarm, or verbally abuse another person.

HEARSAY.　Secondhand information. You needn't repeat what others have told you, as you have no way of knowing the truth of their statements. However, in a deposition you might be asked to name persons who have knowledge of a subject so that they can be deposed.

HOSTILE.　Having the character of an enemy. The term is often applied to a witness from the opposition.

HYPOTHETICAL QUESTION.　A question about an imaginary case similar to the case being considered. The hypothetical question should include all the important and relevant facts of the actual case under consideration.

IMPEACHMENT.　The process of proving a person to be untrustworthy or a liar. Impeachment of physicians can be accomplished by finding inconsistent statements made during long hours of questioning. When inconsistent statements are read before a jury, the physician is made to look dishonest.

INDEPENDENT EXPERT WITNESS.　Not subject to control or influence from another party. To avoid the bias of experts who are hired by each side in a malpractice case, "independent" expert witnesses are sometimes used. If the expert is somehow tied to one party or is "hired for unrelated work" by one party, his independence would be open to question.

IN EVIDENCE.　The facts in evidence are those that have already been shown to be correct. If asked whether a healthy patient would have had the complications your patient had, you might say that the question assumes facts not in evidence because he wasn't initially healthy.

INTERROGATORY.　A list of written questions to be answered in writing under oath. Questions similar to those asked in depositions can be asked, though the opportunity for asking questions requiring investigation is greater with the interrogatory. For example, a surgeon might be asked how many cases of various types he has performed. The lack of opportunity for following up on answers given makes the interrogatory less effective than the deposition. Both methods of discovery are often used in the same case.

INTIMIDATION.   To purposely deter another from action by putting that person in fear. Some plaintiff's attorneys feel that intimidation is an important part of taking a deposition.

INVASION OF PRIVACY.   The unwarranted publicizing of private affairs with which the public has no legitimate concern. Or the wrongful intrusion into one's private activities in such a manner as would cause an ordinary person mental suffering or humiliation. See *Defamation, Libel, Slander.*

LEADING QUESTION.   One that puts words into your mouth or instructs you how to answer.

LEGAL THEORY.   The reasoning, based on statutes and case precedents, that supports an action.

LIBEL.   Defamation caused by writing or signs. See *Slander, Defamation.*

LIKELY.   Something that occurs more often than not, more that 50 percent of the time. See also *Possible, Probable.*

MAGISTRATE.   A public civil officer. U.S. magistrates have some, but not all, of the powers of a judge. A magistrate may decide whether or not a deposition question must be answered. If many conflicts arise during a deposition, the deposition may be held in the presence of a magistrate so that immediate rulings on disagreements can be made.

MALICE.   The performance of a wrongful act with evil intent, and without just cause or excuse, designed to inflict injury on another. The information needed to prove malice might be obtained from the depositions of various persons with knowledge of your patient and his lawsuit. See *Malicious-Prosecution Lawsuit.*

MALICIOUS-PROSECUTION LAWSUIT.   It claims that a physician was sued with malice and for no good reason. A number of facts need to be proved to support the claim of malicious prosecution. The proof can sometimes be obtained by making sure that the depositions of the physician and of other parties document the necessary information. The facts that must be proved to support a claim of malicious prosecution are: (1) a judicial proceeding has been initiated or continued by the patient against the physician, (2) the physician prevailed in this proceeding, (3) there was no probable cause to institute the proceeding, (4) the proceeding was instituted because of malice, and (5) the physician sustained injury.

See also *Damage, Special Damages, Probable Cause, Malice.*

MALPRACTICE. An act of negligence on the part of a health-care practitioner. Four requirements must be satisfied if malpractice is to be proved: (1) the practitioner must have had a *duty* to the patient, (2) the practitioner *breached* that duty, (3) there were *damages* to the patient, and (4) the practitioner's breach of duty was a *proximate cause* of those damages. See *Negligence.*

MATERIAL. Something that's important.

NARRATIVE ANSWER. One in which the witness speaks without interruption. The usual question-and-answer format is put aside. When being sued for malpractice, you're not required to answer questions that require a narrative answer, such as "Tell me everything you know about the patient."

NEGLIGENCE. The failure to do something that a reasonable man would do, or the doing of a thing that a reasonable and prudent man wouldn't do. As applied to medical malpractice, negligence is acting (or failing to act) in the manner a reasonable, prudent, average practitioner of similar standing would act. See also *Gross Negligence.*

NONVERBALS. Gestures, facial expressions, and other actions that communicate meaning. A large part of communication isn't what is said, but how it is said. Nonverbals can intimidate during depositions. It doesn't matter what a person is saying if he has an angry look on his face, is shaking his fist, and is moving toward you.

NUISANCE. An unwarranted or unlawful activity that leads to annoyance and damages to another. A term often applied to medical malpractice cases. See *Frivolous.*

OBJECTION. A statement that one believes the ongoing process (such as a question) is illegal or improper. In many instances, especially during depositions, the process continues or the question must be answered. However, the making of an objection sets the stage for later debate on the legality of the issue. For example, if your attorney doesn't object to an improper question, he may not later be able to keep your answer to the question from being read in court.

OFF THE RECORD. During a deposition, a conversation may be held "off the record." If all attorneys present agree that the conversation should be off the record, the reporter will probably not record the conversation. However, it's still permissible that after the conversation is held, the plaintiff's attorney recite the contents of the conversation onto the record and into the deposition transcript. One should therefore hold off-the-record conversations where they can't be heard.

OUTRAGE. Affront, insult, and abuse. One type of countersuit is the outrage suit. The requirements for an outrage suit are: (1) the outrageous conduct was intentional or reckless, (2) the conduct offended generally accepted standards of decency and morality, and (3) the conduct caused severe emotional distress.

PERJURY. Knowingly making a false statement under oath. Perjury can be claimed if you make contradictory statements in your deposition.

PLAINTIFF. A person who brings an action. The former patient who sues a physician for malpractice is referred to as the plaintiff. This person is no longer a patient and should not be thought of as one; he or she is an opponent in a lawsuit.

PLEADINGS. The formal statements of claims and defenses made by both parties in a lawsuit. These are written documents and may include the complaint, answer, reply to a counterclaim, answer to a cross-claim, third-party complaint, and third-party answer.

POSSIBLE. Capable of happening. Some events are extremely unlikely, but still possible. Questioning is often designed to confuse the interpretation of words such as "possible." See *Likely, Probable*.

PRECEDENT. A decision of a court that furnishes example or authority for a similar case afterwards. Courts are somewhat obligated to follow decisions made in similar previous cases. This is especially true if the decision was in the same state. The higher the court, the more weight the decision carries. For example, supreme courts have more authority than appellate courts. It's important to know about precedents before your deposition.

PRIMA FACIE. At first sight; presumably.

PRIMA FACIE CASE. An argument that will prevail unless new evidence is brought to the contrary.

PRIMA FACIE TORT. Intentionally inflicting damages without excuse or justification by acts that would otherwise be lawful.

PRIVILEGE. A right or exception before the law. For example, the right to keep secret the information discussed with one's attorney or physician. See *Confidential*.

PROBABLE. Something that occurs more than 50 percent of the time. It occurs more often than not. See *Likely, Possible*.

PROBABLE CAUSE. Having more evidence for than against. Probable cause for initiating a malpractice suit is usually recognized to exist when an expert witness testifies in a deposition that negligence did occur.

PROTECTIVE ORDER. An order of the court that protects a person from further discovery, harassment, or other actions.

REFRESHING RECOLLECTION OR MEMORY. The law allows for one to refresh one's memory. A person must consult a source of knowledge that was previously known to him when refreshing his memory. Many rules and correct ways of referring to the refreshing of one's memory have evolved.

RELEVANT. Bearing upon or connected with the matter at hand; pertinent.

RES IPSA LOQUITUR. "The thing speaks for itself." A claim that no expert witness or expert testimony is needed to help decide a case. The facts are so simple that the average layman can figure out what happened. For example, a person with a wart has an anesthetic so that the wart can be removed. He has a cardiac arrest during anesthesia and suffers brain damage. In such a case the doctrine of res ipsa loquitur might be invoked. The defense may claim that the doctrine doesn't apply, and a court case over that preliminary question might ensue.

SETTLEMENT. The closing of a dispute in which differences are adjusted, often by the payment of money. See *Good Faith.*

SLANDER. Defamation by the spoken word. See also *Defamation, Libel.*

SPECIAL DAMAGES. Damages not usually suffered. Special damages are defined differently in various states. Some courts have held that a physician can't recover damages resulting from a frivolous lawsuit unless the damages are different from those usually suffered in a malpractice lawsuit. Thus, it wouldn't be possible to recover damages from losses such as defamation of character, mental distress, increased insurance rates, and attorney's fees. One's deposition can document various forms of insult and harassment that might not be considered usual. See *Damage.*

SPECIAL INJURY. Deprivation of liberty or property. Some courts have not held as special injury humiliation, embarrassment, emotional anguish, subjection to public scorn, ridicule, injury to reputation, and increased liability insurance premiums.

SPECULATION. Theorizing about a matter you really don't know about. In a deposition, you're not required to speculate about anything, and you shouldn't speculate. It's normal to feel a need to speculate when questioned repeatedly about a matter, but such questioning is an effort to cause you to make inaccurate statements. Unless you wish to be proved a liar, don't speculate.

STATUTE OF LIMITATIONS. A limit to the time in which a lawsuit must be filed. For example, in many states a malpractice suit must be filed within two years of when the alleged negligence took place.

The statute of limitations is extended in many states by various rules. For example, the foreign-body rule may extend the statute in cases involving a foreign body (piece of needle, pacemaker, or IUD). If the case involved a minor, the time might be extended until the child becomes an adult.

STATUTORY LAW.   Laws passed by the legislature. See also *Common Law*.

STIPULATIONS.   Agreements made by opposing attorneys on matters they're able to decide. During depositions, this can include the manner of making objections, verifying the accuracy of the deposition transcript, and the need for signing the deposition transcript. Some attorneys will ask their opponent if he agrees to "the usual stipulations". An agreement is sometimes obtained without it being clear what the usual stipulations are. In such a situation, the physician witness should ask what has been agreed to and refuse to proceed until he has been told.

SUBPOENA.   An order to appear at a certain time and place. A subpoena duces tecum orders the production of papers and other evidence.

SUMMONS.   A paper used to start a lawsuit (civil action) and acquire jurisdiction over a person. A sheriff or other officer often notifies the person of the summons. The summons will often say that the person has 30 days to answer the complaint that has been filed. In practice, the person will obtain an attorney who will answer the summons but not immediately answer all charges made in the complaint.

SUPERVISOR.   One who controls another. In some situations, a person will be held responsible for the acts of people he supervises.

TESTIMONY.   Evidence given under oath or affirmation. Other types of evidence come from writings and exhibits.

THEORY.   See *Legal Theory*.

THIRD PARTY.   A person who didn't take part in a transaction. For example, a physician is a third party when a patient and lawyer decide to sue the physician. The responsibility of the patient's lawyer to act reasonably toward the physician has increased in some jurisdictions in the last few years.

TORT.   A private or civil wrong or injury (beside breach of contract). Usually a tort is handled by an action for damages (attempt to get money to right the wrong). See also *Civil*. The elements of every tort action (including a malpractice action) are: (1) existence of legal duty from defendant to plaintiff, (2) a breach of that duty, and (3) damage as a proximate result of the breach of duty.

TRANSCRIPT.   A written record. See *Deposition Transcript*.

VICARIOUS LIABILITY.   Liability for the acts of others. A physician might be held liable for the negligence of his employees. The physician might also be held responsible for the acts of nurses and others employed by a hospital who are under his supervision. The degree of responsibility often depends on how closely the nurse was supervised, whether or not the physician was present at the time of the alleged negligence, and other factors.

WAIVER.   Voluntarily giving up a right, such as the right to verify the accuracy of your deposition transcript.

WILLFUL OR WANTON MISCONDUCT.   A reckless disregard for the safety of others. Willful or wanton misconduct is the failure to exercise ordinary care to prevent injury to a person who should be known to be in danger because of the act being performed.

INDEX